Karen Mav
14th Octobe

Priesthood and Society

Priesthood and Society

KENNETH MASON

Second Edition

CANTERBURY
PRESS
Norwich

All rights reserved. No part of this publication may be reproduced, stored in a retrieval system, or transmitted, in any form or by any means, electronic, mechanical, photocopying or otherwise, without the prior permission of the publisher, Canterbury Press

Text © Kenneth Mason 1992, 2002

First published in 1992 by the Canterbury Press Norwich
(A publishing imprint of Hymns Ancient & Modern Limited, a registered charity)
St Mary's Works, St Mary's Plain
Norwich, Norfolk, NR3 3BH
This new edition published in 2002

Kenneth Mason has asserted his right under the Copyright, Design and Patents Act, 1988, to be identified as the Author of this Work

British Library Cataloguing in Publication data

A catalogue record for this book is available from the British Library

ISBN 1-85311-4693

Typeset by Rowland Phototypesetting Ltd,
Bury St Edmunds, Suffolk
Printed and bound in Great Britain by
Biddles Ltd, Guildford and King's Lynn

DEDICATION

To Barbara, Andrew & Elaine,
who have patiently borne
the necessity of my priesthood.

Contents

Acknowledgements ix
Preface to the Second Edition xi

1. The Necessity of Priesthood
1. A Parable 1
2. The Rudiments of Priesthood 3
3. Official Priesthood 7
4. Necessity and Impossibility 11
5. Christ, the Fulfilment of Priesthood 17

2. The Universal Moment – Priesthood and Ministry in the New Testament
1. The Gospel as Re-evaluation 23
2. The Nature of the New Testament Witness 25
3. The Content of the New Testament Witness 29

3. Towards Definition – A Christian Sacral Priesthood
1. The Constantinian Opportunity 40
2. The Eucharistic Priesthood 47

4. Priesthood and the Subversive Gospel
1. Contradiction 57
2. Anti-Structure 59
3. Christian Anti-Structure 67

5. Priesthood, Symbol and Doctrine
1. The Ministries 'of Angels and Men' 73
2. The Symbol of Love 77
3. Ministry as the Carrier of Doctrine 82

6. The Living Symbol
1. The Symbolic form of the Ministry 87
(a) Consecratory Intention 87

(b) Human Beings as Symbols 88
(c) Doctrinal Congruence 89
2. The Representation of God in Christ 90
3. Common Membership in the Body 96
4. Sacramental Action 101
5. The Principle of Grace 106
6. Institution and Function 110

7. The Emergence of the Laity
1. Holy Drudgery 114
2. Luther and the Laity 119
3. Constructive Revolution 124

8. Secularisation and the Church's Priesthood
1. The Nature of the Change 129
2. Consequences for the Church 139
(a) The Triviality of Faith 139
(b) The Introversion of the Church 140
(c) The Ecclesiastical Seduction of the Laity 142

9. Priestly Askesis Today
1. Learned Obedience 148
2. Taken from among human beings in things pertaining to God 149
3. In all things like unto his brothers and sisters 153
4. In the midst of the congregation 158
5. Made Perfect 163

Notes 167
Index of Subjects 173
Index of Names 176

Acknowledgements

I wish to acknowledge the use of published material as follows:
Part of Martin Luther's *Greater Catechism*, reprinted from THE BOOK OF CONCORD, edited by T. G. Tappert, copyright © 1959 Fortress Press, used by permission of Augsburg Fortress.
From *The Shape of the Liturgy* by Dom Gregory Dix, reprinted by permission of A. & C. Black, Publishers.
From *Revelations of Divine Love* by Julian of Norwich, translated by J. Walsh SJ, used by permission of Burns & Oates Ltd.
From *Collected Poems 1909–1962* by T. S. Eliot, and from *The Anathemata*, *The Sleeping Lord*, and *Epoch & Artist*, by David Jones, used by permission of Faber & Faber Ltd.
From *A Theology of Auschwitz* by Ulrich Simon, published by V. Gollancz Ltd, and used by permission of the author.
From *A Celebration of Faith* by Austin Farrer, by permission of Hodder & Stoughton Ltd.
From *The Problem of Multiple Realities: Alfred Schutz & Robert Musil* by Peter Berger, in M. Natanson (ed.), *Phenomenology & Social Reality, Essays in Memory of Alfred Schutz*, Evanston, Northwestern University Press, 1970, reprinted by permission of Kluwer Academic Publishers.
From *The Gospel and the Catholic Church*, by A. M. Ramsey, used by permission of the Longman Group, UK.
From *Later Poems, 1972–1982* by R. S. Thomas, used by permission of Macmillan London Ltd.
From *The Poems of Gerard Manley Hopkins*, 4th Edition, edited by W. H. Gardner and N. H. MacKenzie, and published by the Oxford University Press.
From *Principles of Christian Theology* (Revised Edition 1977) by John Macquarrie, used by permission of SCM Press Ltd.

Biblical quotations are best described as 'author's version'. They are based on the Revised Version, published jointly by the Oxford & Cambridge University Presses, but adapted to modern idiom.

I wish to thank Doris Taylor, Rosemary Procter and Margaret Young for undertaking the typing of my manuscript, and to express my gratitude to those clergy groups and students who have listened to so much of the material presented here and helped me develop it through their comments and discussion.

I owe a particular debt to the British Trust for the Oecumenical Institute for Advanced Theological Studies, for a bursary which enabled me to take a sabbatical term at the Institute at Tantur, Jerusalem, in 1983, and to my colleagues there who in so many ways assisted my studies at that time.

KENNETH MASON
All Saints, 2001

Preface to the Second Edition

As I write this, the world is still seeking an adequate response to the violence of September 11th 2001. Inchoate emotion may eventually lead to determinate, rational and transparent action, but it does not yet appear what that will be. Having spent a good deal on saying goodbye to the twentieth century, people seem determined to play its tunes over again, only louder, beginning as in June 1914 with an act of terrorist protest. Many commentators have spoken of September 11th in apocalyptic terms, unavoidably, one might think, given the pictures of smoke rising over the great city, but few as yet have dared to take the obvious next step and speak of judgement. Nevertheless, that seems to be where we are, not that the terrorists' acts were themselves a judgement except in their own eyes, but rather because anything done in response will be so momentous that we shall be invoking judgement on ourselves in doing it. What we sow we shall certainly reap. Politicians are using words like *freedom*, *civilisation*, *democracy*, and *peace-loving*. In the context, these are holy words intended to sanctify the cause that uses them, but they are also holy enough in themselves to rebound on those who use them unworthily. The whole system that is now organising itself to defend itself will be judged in the means it uses to do so.

That means more particularly, that the priesthoods of our culture are under judgement, taking *priesthood* in the generic sense of any body of people who represent the fundamental bases of society to it. Religious leaders cannot absolve themselves of this responsibility, but neither can the politicians, the media of news and entertainment (increasingly hard to distinguish), and the personalities and celebrities who seem to exist only within those media and whose free-spending hedonism resonates so perfectly with the needs of our economy.

It could properly be expected that a book on priesthood and society should attempt some social criticism, and I chose to base mine on a thesis about the trivial or illusory freedom of individuals in secularised society. After ten years I think this is still a useful and accurate approach. It is true that concerted action by charities and individuals has made some difference to the way governments perceive third-world debt, though the recent tendency for such action to carry a nihilist fringe is not encouraging and overall it seems true still that individuals are alienated from government and suspicious of politicians, and that religion is so much a private matter that it is not – must not – be allowed to affect public policy. These are symptoms of a vast split between public and private concern, so vast that we may wonder whether our civilisation is not held together by ignorance and illusion. The general anxiety that our rulers are not telling us the truth is all of a piece with a fear that they might do so.

When the situation becomes as disastrous as it seems it may, disillusionment is bound to follow, and people will ask again whether there is something solid on which they can build their lives. The priesthood that seeks to meet this challenge will have to show itself to be wise, compassionate and not exploitative. A tested and proved integrity will be its chief characteristic.

And this is where it becomes necessary to speak about God, and not merely about religion and priesthood. Apart from God these things reveal a great deal about human nature, but otherwise they are only systems without substance. It is God, as the one who justifies us by his grace, who can give integrity to those who could never in honesty claim it for themselves. It is God alone who is able to overcome the contradiction that otherwise is bound to defeat every attempt on the part of humanity to provide a priesthood for itself.

Priesthood is necessary as a witness to the solid ground of human existence together. It is also unattainable, because this ground is God, and none of us is adequate to represent him. We can only take up this impossible vocation if we are assured that God has overcome the contradiction involved, as he did when he turned our enmity against himself into the means by which we could be released from it.

Those who go beyond reading a book and find ways of making use of it are its most eloquent critics. Since this book was first published my tasks as a teacher and examiner have put me in the way of a number of references to it in students' essays. All, I think have seen it as a defence of the institution of ordained ministry in the church, and that is fair enough because I firmly believe that a church without institutions is an incoherent idea, however attractive. What has been less recognised is that I want to defend only a particular kind of institution – one which can coexist with a powerful anti-structural impulse, and which is not opposed to many of the activities which lead to protests against 'institutionalism'. Among these might be the freedom and power of the Christian laity to take the initiative in the service of God's kingdom without further accreditation, and so to realise the restoration of priestliness to every man and woman in Christ. And chief among them is the freedom of the Spirit of God to make the symbols and traditions of the church transparent to glory, and so move us closer to that transparency ourselves. I firmly believe that the institutional priesthood of the church, in its symbolic and sacramental calling, does not inhibit these things, and is given to make them more accessible to us.

Compassion too, although highly esteemed in our culture, really lies beyond us. Those who advertise it most vigorously seem unable to detach it from the advertisement of themselves. Like all forms of publicity, it attracts suspicion. Our need is for a compassion which is completely self-effacing, and that seems to be offered to us only in the way God himself responds to our suffering by taking it on himself and hiding himself in it.

Since this book was first published the ordination of women has been accepted in the Anglican Churches of the British Isles. I welcome this development, and have revised the language of the book to take account of it.

It is well known however that the [illegible] the moon. He is forbidden to do [illegible] to be your companion on the way to [illegible] which you must take for yourself, but that he is [illegible] when you come out, if in fact you have decided [illegible] get you back home again.

And the likeness to a priest lies precisely then in the [illegible] that disability. There are incidental features in the story [illegible] on to confirm this. The life has a dangerous, [illegible] which could only be sustained by some inner compulsion. The stalker's family relations are strained: his wife [illegible] has married, and the children are famous for [illegible] people react strangely to him – admiration, fear, [illegible] together. They may or may not want to go [illegible] with him, but even for those who stay put [illegible] He reminds you that the world does not end at the [illegible] beyond it lies the possibility of a vast change, [illegible]

CHAPTER ONE

The Necessity of Priesthood

'. . . the way to the chambers of destruction is a priestly possibility.'

Ulrich Simon, *A Theology of Auschwitz*

1. A Parable

The Russian film, *Stalker*, directed by Andrei Tarkovsky, is a parable of priesthood.

The story begins in some decrepit corner of a ruined civilisation. Out beyond the fence and the border-guards there is a deserted land where no one is meant to go. The weeds grow tall and tangled, and there are no obvious paths. You can hear the woodpecker drumming and the cuckoo calling, but otherwise it is all silence. Somewhere out there – it may be only a little way, for it is not the physical distance that matters – is a house, and in the house a room in which you can state your deepest wish and you will have it. A stalker is someone who can get you into that room.

It is well known however that the stalker himself never goes into the room. He is forbidden to do so. His business is to guide you, to be your companion on the way, to point you to the final step which you must take for yourself, but then to go no further. Then when you come out, if in fact you have decided to go in, he will get you back home again.

And the likeness to a priest lies precisely there, in that limitation, that disability. There are incidental features in the story which go on to confirm this. The life has a dangerous, disturbed quality, which could only be sustained by some inner compulsion. The stalker's family relations are strained, his wife wonders what she has married, and the children are famous for their oddity. In society people react strangely to him – admiration, fear, distaste, mingled together. They may or may not want to go out beyond the fence with him, but even for those who stay put, he stands for something. He reminds you that the world does not end at the fence, and that beyond it lies the possibility of a vast change. He is a symbol of hope, even to those who do not want to act on hope. He points to a connection between this constrained existence and something else, elusive but free. And yet he has never made the connection himself. For him the connection is impossible, and he cannot be a stalker unless he lives with this impossibility.

On the surface the story is a fairy tale, like the one about your fairy godmother who offers you three wishes, though here with one important difference, that in this case there is only one. Three wishes is definitely better, not because you can get more out of them, but because there is a safety in three which is not there in one. When you have three you can use the second to cancel the first if you need to do so, and then the third can be kept in reserve. Here there is only the third. There is no scope for experiment, no allowance for second thoughts. Perhaps, then, the stalker is a dealer in magic who cannot himself become a magician. If he entered the room he might claim the right to grant wishes himself. Perhaps only a stalker knows how to make such a claim, and so supplant the power that inhabits the room by taking its virtue away with him. Then he would no longer point to it, but be it. A priest, we might think, can never become a god, exercising divine power in the everyday world. He is there to serve the god by pointing to him, not to control him, and he is not to be identified with him even when the pressure of his office seems to require that he should.

Or, we might say, it has to do with sacrifice, with extreme self-restraint for the sake of others. Suppose there is a law that those who enter the room can never even approach it again, then the stalker cannot claim the privilege which the room offers because he could never again give it to others. It may offer a way of escape which, if he takes it, no one else will ever be able to take.

But we are to find, as the story unfolds, that in truth no one ever takes it. Just at the point where a wish might be made, second thoughts intervene. Each and all faced with the prospect of making their wish decline it and then go back to the decrepit world from which they had set out. And if things are different after that it is not that they have wished them to be different. They have decided not to make a wish at all. In the film this decision – this essential refusal – is made almost at the end, and we switch immediately to the stalker coming home to his wife. The return journey does not matter. There are no dangers or potential confusions on it that could be compared with those faced on the outward journey. Once the decision is made the story is really over. The story is about the decision itself – the decision that everyone has to make on the threshold of that room, either that they will not enter it, or that if they do they will ask for nothing. For who can trust himself to command the power of the universe?

One possible response to that question is to say that there is no such power, and no one needs to think of commanding it. Even at the door of the room, after the journey has already been made, that is a possible answer. Another is to recognise that the question has searched you out beyond your ability to answer it. You are a worm and not human, and all you can do is resign yourself to the mercy of whatever has questioned you. Yet another is to take note of what you now know of the depth of your own responsibility, and to take your sense of responsibility back with you. In fairy stories you are always held to the consequence of whatever you wish for even if you blunder into it. In this story you are at least allowed to reflect before you wish. Magic is best kept unused. Men should work within the limits of their own wisdom. It is not that you cannot devise a way to make yourself God, but that you will lose your human dignity in doing so. For God's sake, who gave it to you, you should not put that dignity at risk.

In any case, the stalker has to live with a sense of incapacity, of impossibility. Part of his calling is to be known as a certain kind of person, but he knows that if his public reputation were simply true he would not be the person he is.

2. The Rudiments of Priesthood

It is not easy to pin the idea of priesthood down. When we look at official institutional forms of priesthood we find them differing, even in the same society. In ancient Israel, for example, there were people called priests and people called prophets, and each group had its sub-divisions. And though it is possible to confront their callings one with another, in a more distant perspective they are very much alike. From the point of view of social anthropology both priest and prophet count as 'religious functionaries' or 'sacral persons'.[1] No matter how different their behaviour may be, both of them articulate the relation between God and society, both act as living signs of his presence, both are expected to interpret life in the light of his character. Fundamental to their office is a recognised relationship with God which they enter upon for the sake of other people. At the same time the way they work out this relationship is never entirely settled, and can always be adapted to new circumstances. The phenomenon appears to have a clear enough centre, but diffuse edges.

We should not aim at greater precision than this before we have followed up this perception of diffuseness. Before we try to become exact about priesthood we must recognise the limits of exactitude. It may be part of the task of an official priesthood to make its own competence clear to the people it serves, but there is also a widely shared, general experience of priesthood that has to be recognised before official priesthood can be fully explained. There is a natural and universal priesthood which is inevitably diffuse in its outlines, but which provides the background against which institutional priesthood stands out. Official priesthoods, with their precise tasks and high claims, represent a concentration or making explicit of activities that human beings share in universally.

Think of two lovers writing to one another daily. What does this mean to them? They seem to be exchanging information but it is probably a very private sort of information, relevant to nothing except the love they share. Really it is love itself they are communicating, not by writing about it explicitly (they may be too clumsy or too embarrassed to do that) but by acting it out in the exchange of letters. The letters are a means of communication, a shared possession, a sign of mutual belonging. The two who write them are performing an act of reassurance for one another, celebrating a ritual which is peculiarly theirs, and so affirming their membership of one another. We could say (and not in the manner of a mere metaphor, but by a true analogy) that they have become priests to one another who celebrate a personal sacrament.

Families too develop their rituals of belonging and their sacraments of assurance. We see this in the way stories and nursery rhymes are shared with little children. They are not just passed on; they find their proper occasions. In a more varied way, certain recurrent events are made to stand out – bedtime, the beginnings of new seasons as when the first frost appears, rainy days, birthdays, the night before Christmas. Parents take up mysterious and evocative roles toward their children. They play at Santa Claus, or they assist the fairies who exchange discarded teeth for coins under the pillow. These things are much more than 'idle' play, more than the passing on of interesting folklore or the reliving of one's own childhood, more even than complaisance with the child's demand to 'say it again'. These things are not simply injected into life. They are an interpretation of it. They are there to show that diverse occasions have their meaning, and that strange events are not wholly strange. There is a covenant of promise that comprehends them all. When parents play solemn games and call up old memories for their children they are showing them that the world into which they have come is dependable. Even the disturbing things, the surprises, hurts and distresses, have been provided for. How otherwise could a mother kiss her children's bruises better! The virtue of the kiss lies in the one who gives it, and the assurance with which it is given. The act is priestly as much as medicinal, as aboriginal medicine often is.

Growing up doesn't put an end to this kind of personal transaction, though the need for it may become more complex and the way it is obtained more subtle. People continue throughout their lives to feel the need for someone who will play the parent's part for them. This is not of course likely to be the most explicit element in what happens. People seldom say directly to others, 'I want you to mother me for a bit.' The childlike longing hides itself within a request for factual information or practical help, as when we call in a plumber or mechanic or ask a doctor for diagnosis and treatment. In each of these cases (and not only in the case of the doctor where the parental and priestly element is often obvious), we are appealing to something more than instrumental skill. We want someone who has knowledge to put a name to the unknown mystery we face, we want someone competent to draw a boundary to our anxiety, we want the reliability of the world to be reaffirmed at a time when we are feeling perplexed and uncertain. We want to know that something which we do not understand ourselves is nevertheless understood by someone – that is lies within the bounds of rationality and is not to be taken as the first sign of the break-up of the world.

Anyone who stands beside me in my uncertainty in this way can be seen, psychologically, as a surrogate parent and socially as a kind of priest. At its most rudimentary level there need be nothing official about this, nothing organised or even understood. All I need is that someone senses that my world would be a better world for me if he or she took up this momentary role. Let the familiar words be said, the common opinion be reasserted that I had begun to doubt – that will usually be enough. If he or she does something, it will be all the better the more normal and apparently utilitarian it is. Only from within my anxiety will it appear as a comforting ritual.

Again, parents have to be reconcilers among their children, and that is not something that can be done merely by punishing those who start fighting. It isn't the putting down of wickedness but the lifting up of spirits that reconciles. Simply to offer people a chance to share fun may do the trick, as Boswell discovered when he contrived that Wilkes and Johnson should meet at a dinner party. The child shut up in his own resentment has to be helped to emerge into a wider world. So in adult life, when people call in a mediator, they are tacitly acknowledging that their quarrel concerns other people beside themselves, and that they owe it to themselves as well as to those others to let them have a voice in the affair. We need to see our particular concern as part of a wider whole, and to let ourselves be addressed and persuaded from the standpoint of the whole.

Here then are some of the constituents of priesthood diffused through daily social life: to rehearse promises by word or sign, to bring assurance to those in need of healing, to reconcile those who stand apart, and to affirm the ways in which we belong to one another, to interpret chance happenings as part of a rational order and to meet emergencies with hope. All of these things belong to priesthood. Of course they also belong to men and women as such. If these things are priestly then there is a diffuse, rudimentary and largely unnoticed element of priesthood in much human behaviour. But if that diffuse priesthood of all humankind were not there, then the rise of explicit and official priesthoods would be much less comprehensible and perhaps rather more sinister than it is. If people are prepared to accept the definite claims and overt rituals of organised priesthoods, may it not be that they are disposed to do this because they already receive a similar kind of ministry from their fellow human beings, however much less obvious it usually is? Official priesthood stands out from the diffuse and rudimentary priesthood of humanity by its organised character, but its roots are in humanity itself.

But how then does the transition take place from this natural, shared, implicit priesthood to explicitly recognised historical institutions?

3. Official Priesthood

'Ideas,' says Peter Berger, 'require social resonance to attain and to retain their plausibility'.[2] Unless other people act upon the convictions that we act upon, they cease to be convictions. Unless our basic moral position is given to us, and given back to us in experience with other people, we lose it.

What we have seen so far is that people offer this kind of resonance to one another in ways which are relatively intuitive. Nevertheless we should not think that they have no institutional character at all. There is a tradition, unreflective though it is, behind those activities. There can be, if not premeditation, a moment of deliberation before one acts. We have learned what is useful in those situations by a kind of acquired instinct of which we can become aware. Actions of this kind have it in them to become more definite in their aims and more recognisable for what they are – to become the activities of an official priesthood. We can see official priesthood as a coalescence in a social institution of the elements of diffused priesthood, like globules in cream coalescing to become butter.

So when we consider institutional priesthoods like the ancient Israelite priesthood, or the priesthood of the Christian Church, or the pagan priesthoods which in some ways lie behind both, we should not think of their members as totally distinct from other people in society. Rather they bring a heightened definition to something which is general. It is this defining, rather than something uniquely theirs, which gives them their character as sacral and institutional persons with a firm tradition of their own.

Priesthood receives its institutional character by way of the constant and reiterated expectations that grow up around it. Organisations emerge out of demands and hopes, regularly expressed, seeking fulfilment. So it is here. A group of people become the focus of loyalties and assurances which work their way out through the whole of a society. Individuals, of course, can become the centre of a personal network of others who look to them for help. Every village, every large office or team of workers, is likely to have someone in it who stands out as a moral resource to the rest. This is personal and uncovenanted. With an official priesthood people know that they can expect certain things – even demand them – of members of the priesthood, merely because they are members. Personal familiarity is not necessary in these cases. The institution itself already conveys enough knowledge to encourage the appropriate action.

It is an acknowledged sense of competence, then, that keeps an institutional priesthood in business. Just as doctors, plumbers and mechanics are felt to be competent to meet certain recurring emergencies and perennial needs, so it is with priests. The difference lies in the peculiar nature of those needs – in the way priests minister to moral confidence, and to the conviction that the venture of life is worthwhile. This is a very general, fundamental question, although there are particular occasions when it is felt with special force. Why is it that, not merely among Christians, certain occasions in life seem to require a special sacral recognition, and call for the ministry of a priest? There are the obvious ones like birth, death and marriage and others almost as obvious – personal emergencies like the onset of puberty, the taking up of new responsibilities, or the experience of injury and illness; there are also shared emergencies like natural disaster or the beginning of a war. What these all have in common is that no one can meet them in the strength of a merely technical ability. The question is rather one of justification, of self-confidence, of entering upon something fresh in the assurance that, whether it succeeds or fails, it is right to try. At these moments the resonance of ideas, of which Berger speaks, is most in question and most in need of a deliberate answer. And beyond these moments, each of which raises a particular question in our minds, there is an overall and total question to be answered. The whole human project poses the same problem in a massive way. How do people establish that their life has a consistent direction and a worthwhile goal? The special competence of priesthood is its ability to handle that sort of question.

Institutional priesthoods are always associated with some definite tradition – that is to say, a characteristic collection of ideas and actions which has been handed on from the past. There can be no invented priesthoods. That is not to say that new priesthoods do not appear in society, but their newness lies in a new relation between society and something already there, perceived as already 'old'. When the office of kingship (which is itself a form of priesthood)[3] was adopted in Israel, it was so partly as a development of the office of the judges, and partly as an imitation of something already well known in other nations. Or when, in the Roman Empire, civic religion declined and was augmented in people's attention by a variety of oriental cults, part of the appeal of the new religions was that they spoke with a more primitive voice, to human concerns perceived as more enduring.

Further, the tradition which a priesthood represents has to be so distinctive in content yet so rich in potential that it requires a special group of people to take responsibility for it. There is no special priesthood to serve the tradition of common sense. What everybody knows is no one's particular competence. It is in recognition of this that, although the Christian churches have developed institutional priesthoods, they continue to assert that every member of the church is priestly. Christian faith is by nature open to all. There are no esoteric secrets in it. Nevertheless, here as elsewhere, a need is felt for a special proficiency in handling what is common to all, a special guardianship over shared tradition. Priests work at those points where a specific tradition meets the varied circumstances of human life, and there they serve as interpreters, expressing the relevance of the one to the other and offering people a fresh perception of both. There are skills in this which are not common to everyone, habits of mind and feeling that develop within the office and are not likely to flourish outside it. Even a totally priestly people, then, may have its own particular priests.

There are other occupations in society which require skills in handling a particular tradition – law, medicine, and finance for example. Priesthood is distinctive here because of the symbolic character of its traditions. Priests as such are not concerned to get things done, to make and distribute goods, to fix deals and repair breakages. Their skills are not instrumental. Rather they have to call upon the symbols available to them to minister, as we have seen, to private and public confidence. They are to help people answer the question, 'What's the point?' That question is not answered by logical explanation or by undertaking to do the job for the questioner. It is only answered, for those to whom it is a real question, by bringing them to a new ordering of their perceptions and emotions, to a new symbolic understanding of the world in which they are set. When people are struggling against a sense of waste and failure, through the perplexity of deep suffering, through the shock of sudden loss or the threat of losing possession of themselves, nothing will restore confidence to them but the sense of a new *cosmos* in which to live. Priesthood is concerned with initiating and maintaining existence in such a *cosmos*.[4]

Priesthood therefore communicates through symbols, and priests themselves normally become part of the language of symbolic communication. The priests' own persons, not their personality alone, but their setting in the community, become the most significant word they speak. Priests are more than custodians of symbolic ideas. They have to act out, and live out the symbols which are central to their tradition. They come to represent those symbols in their dress and behaviour, like living icons. They articulate, through their own words and actions, the relationship between society and its sacred things. That is why the priestly life is always in some way a ceremonial life. The natural and basic form for such an articulation is not detailed exposition, not lecturing or preaching, however fascinating and somehow necessary that may be. It is ritual.

The principal distinguishing mark of an institutional priesthood is its sacral character, its standing within the field of the sacred. There are systems of ideas immanent in society which are not sacred, even though important. Those are the business of pseudo-priesthoods, the propagandists of ideologies and the maintenance experts of the national way of life. True sacral priesthoods represent ideas which are held to be, in some sense, bestowed upon society from beyond itself. They are not human possessions but divine gifts. Society cannot itself provide a ground for its own deepest convictions. It cannot find within itself resonance for the ideas that are to matter most to it. It has to be addressed from outside. Humankind is like a lover who cannot believe that he is loved in return unless his loved one, deliberately and spontaneously, assures him that it is so. Just so, people in society need some unforced recognition from God if their ideas about God are to be held with basic trust.

Priesthood then has to do for all society what various individuals do for others within it, that is, maintain moral security in the face of the threat of dissolution. From one point of view it is society's own spokesman. It represents the whole of a society to its members, gathering up in its traditions all that society finds most significant. From another point of view it has to cut loose from society and show that those things which are most to be valued among men and women are not their own but the gift of God. It is not, then, only that society offers its members a venerable tradition, an ordered world, a common mind. It is also that at the heart of such a system place has to be found for something other, something capable of holding the human edifice together and, if it is taken seriously, also of shattering it to its foundations. Sacred truth derives its sacredness, not from those who share it or who live by it, but from the God whose reality it represents.

Throughout this attempt to describe priesthood I have been aware of a double-sidedness to what I have been saying. I am trying to defend priesthood against its detractors, and I have no intention to debunk it. Yet the account I am offering may sound very like a debunking. It seems that the whole thing can be reduced to a demand for reassurance, first experienced in childhood and continued with ever greater elaboration into adult and organised social life. What then is the claim to sacred truth, we might ask, but the tacit agreement to sustain mutual reassurance to the limit of our imaginative grasp? It may be so. Probably it is so much of the time. The needs which operate here are so powerful that humankind is bound to work out systems of this kind, and provide itself with priesthoods whether justified or not in what they represent. The only check on a totally debunking attitude here is the thought that, in spite of humanity's propensity for making itself gods, a true God may have to be reckoned with, and that if so he may be prepared to meet us within the area broadly covered by priesthood. Admittedly that is an area where idolatry and self-deception are much more likely to be found than truth. But if there is any truth in faith at all, and God is real, then it may be that we can look to him to save us from idolatry and to justify the devices we resort to in our dealings with him, precisely at the point where those devices are deployed. It may be also, though, that the cost of testing this hypothesis is immeasurable.

4. Necessity and Impossibility

We seem to have arrived at a point where everything is to be gained and everything lost, at which the paradoxical character of priesthood as a social institution has become apparent. Hope, in this enterprise, seems to be inseparable from hazard. On the one hand we perceive an ineradicable drive in society to evolve a priesthood. On the other, any attempt to show what priesthood is also shows that it cannot be attained. Priesthood is necessary but impossible, impossible but necessary.

The necessity of priesthood arises out of the social nature of humankind itself. Every individual, every social group, every distinct human identity, needs to be confirmed from beyond itself. Only when it finds that its own ideas are answered by ideas that come to it 'from outside' can it work confidently with those ideas. And so human groups look out for the occasions on which these resonances occur, and seek to give them a predictable, repeatable character. They develop institutions which guard and pass on the fundamental notions of a culture – the sacred ideas, the useful myths, the memories of salvation bestowed in the past which can be taken, in turn, as pledges of salvation in the future. Whatever the character of these institutions, and traditionally they have always been religious, the function they play in society is that of priesthood.

But given this tendency in society, to evolve a priesthood for itself, we still have to ask whether the tendency is beneficial or malignant. Is this the way society is opened up to genuine grace, and human fulfilment is secured? Or is it the way we bring about the worst betrayal of ourselves? Priesthood offers a commerce between the human and the divine, but at the same time warns that this cannot be taken for granted, as though human beings have commerce with the divine 'by nature'. God and humans have to be incommensurate with one another, and though God may measure us against himself he does not do it according to a measure that we already possess. Divine authority must never be reduced to a species of human authority, or it will lose the quality for which human beings seek it. Our human sense of purpose in existence has to rest upon God's claim and call, and not upon something we supply for ourselves. Priesthood has to be, at heart, an appeal to divine authority in the conviction that divine authority does exist and has been given for the human enterprise. And yet how can any human institution really reflect that divine authority?

There is no final answer to that question, short of the end of priesthood itself in some ultimate and total revelation. The risk of idolatry runs along with the whole of human religion, and there is no simple test by which we can distinguish idolatrous priesthoods from those 'called and instituted by God himself'. Of course there is an obvious kind of idolatry – the worship of wood and stone – but no religion seriously invites people to share in that. The ever present danger lies in the subtle idolatries – the perversion of God's grace to make it into a human possession, the conversion of God's truth into a convenient slogan. It is not that God does not reveal himself, but that we debase his revelation by the way we receive it and put it to use.

So priesthood is defined by the seemingly contradictory

demands it has to meet. It has to manifest the coming together of God and humanity without diminishing one or the other. It has to provide a measure of the immeasurable. It has to be separate from the human, for the sake of the God who transcends humanity, yet wholly one with men and women, because it is for their sake that it exists. And it has to be all this, not in some ideal world in which God's will is simply done and all is transparent to his purpose, but in a world in which God's purposes for humankind are untiringly thwarted, often by ourselves.

Priesthood is commonly described as a mediation between God and humanity, or as the Epistle to the Hebrews has it, priests are 'taken from among human beings in things pertaining to God' (Heb. 5.1). They are therefore expected to hold together two realities which, on the very premises which define their calling, are conceived to be separate. They are to represent humanity and represent God without falsifying the image of either, and therefore without becoming a third reality in themselves, different from both. They are to have complete solidarity with their fellows and at the same time be separate from them. Consecration to a sacred calling always involves this double movement, away from humankind yet deeper into it. It separates those called, and invests their life with a distinctive meaning, yet in doing so it reflects back upon the human society from which they are drawn, giving it a sign of God's commitment to it.

Now the priest's separateness has to be shown in some way. He or she is a living symbol, a walking sacrament.[5] The relationships, behaviour, the appearance of priests are bound to be affected by that. They may wear peculiar clothes, cut their hair in a special way, adopt a special 'style', and be known by a distinctive title. They may remain celibate, or if not, their marriage may be invested with special exemplary qualities. Such things encourage the notion that they are not like other people, and are meant to do so.

These marks of priestly separation all come together in the liturgy or cult. What is done in liturgy draws upon other aspects of life and spills over into them again, but it is never simply one with them. And the priest, as the leader of liturgy, is a living sign of discontinuity. He or she has to be this, to function as a priest at all. His or her ritual words have to be heard as words from God; ritual actions have to be seen as acts of God. Cultic actions may draw upon the stuff of common life but they must also go beyond them. The worshipper must not be left saying, 'There is nothing here which is not within my own human power.' Rather he or she must respond, 'Here I cannot help myself. Here I must let God come to me'. And so everything liturgical, and especially the liturgical minister, however common in origin, must be marked with a mark of separation.

Now it is true, as someone may properly object, that at least in Christian thought these harsh dichotomies are ruled out. Christians do not believe that if something comes from us it cannot come from God, nor do they easily accept a sharp separation between priests and others in the fellowship of the Church. It is not only the Christian priest, but every Christian, who is a walking sacrament. Nevertheless this does not mean that the revelation of God's presence is simply reduced to the natural appearance of the world, or to the common features of human life. It is true that the transcendent God has actually given himself to humankind, so that *transcendent* can no longer be taken in the sense of *alien*. Nevertheless it is really *God* who has given himself to humankind, and God is not to be identified with humanity. Speech about God's gift of himself to humankind is not just another way of saying that divinity is a synonym for humanity. And if that is so, and however near God has come, the difference that his coming makes still has to be signified in some way. The sense of separation, in worship and in those who lead it, may be hard to get right, but it is necessary all the same.

But it is hard to get right. The marks of separation in a priest are often seen, not as the consecration of our common humanity but as the draining away of its most vital characteristics. Priestly people are thought of as attenuated, without desires or passions except perhaps for purely religious causes. They do not have feelings as other people have, they are protected against temptation, they are harmless. And these views are not merely false, or unrealistic; they are sinister. When priests are pictured in this way they are being conformed to a scheme of humanity that never was, an ideal that neither could nor should be attained. To set up a false standard of human righteousness, and then to make priests act as surrogates of that righteousness on behalf of everyone else, is to commit a double error in which each half exacerbates the other. It is essentially mistaken to think that we must become angelic in order to be perfect, and it does moral violence to individuals to force them into such a mould.

It seems that the idea of a separated priesthood leads, maybe not necessarily, but with a frightening facility, to a subtle form of idolatry. The priest does not count as human but as a God-substitute. If these attitudes are brought to priesthood and are not held with any kind of irony, then it is right to speak of idolatry. For idolatry is humanity's attachment to itself under the name of God. It is human society's way of protecting its own sense of coherence through the pretence that the devices that hold it together are divine, not human. There is a sense in which any affirmation that is made in the field of religion, if it is made without mitigation, without some sense that it is not for us to make it, is simply an act of human self-assertion. Positive religion has to be released from the spirit of positivism. A faith which is aware of idolatry is always, in one of its modes, a negative faith. It may not smash images, but it distinguishes sharply between the image and what it represents. An Eastern Orthodox worshipper, venerating an icon, does not forget that the icon is made of wood and God is not. In the same way all the paraphernalia of religion, and the distinctive resources of priesthood, have to be viewed with detachment. We may not deny that these things are of our own devising, or that our normal bent is to devise such things in order to protect something within ourselves. Our glories are fragile, our stock of rites and formulae, mythic stories and words of power, is precarious. These things are first of all our own and not God's. The question is whether and how the miracle can happen by which they serve God's purposes. Priests who have had to face this question know at least that the difference between their own ministry and that of a religious charlatan is not one that they themselves can make, but only God. (He that judges me is the Lord, 1 Cor. 4.4.) It is certainly not a doubt that can be answered by an appeal to sincerity. People can be sincerely wrong.

The truth of priesthood, then, does not stand in its positive qualities. And yet the negative approach, that asks, 'with what will you compare God?' cannot give the final answer either. If negativity is the whole of faith, and if God is only 'neither this nor that', then he can reveal himself only in ways that cannot be articulated. Even someone who had received God's gift of himself could not articulate what he had received. And then humanity as social and humanity as believer would have to be torn apart. There could be no continuity in the service of God, no tradition, no sharing, no abiding promise of redemption or apprehension of judgement. If the idea of priesthood, of the consecration of humanity in all its diverse experience, is to have any validity, something positive has to be said or done however obviously human it is.

Priesthood cannot remain itself if it can only demonstrate the Godhead of God by losing touch with humanity. And that must mean that if Godhead and humanity are finally incompatible with one another, priesthood is finally impossible because any human intercourse with God is impossible. Only if God can take up humanity without destroying it can there be fellowship between us and God. Only if God confirms humanity by his gift of himself to men and women can we talk about the consecration of our common life and of our natural abilities. Priesthood has to move nearer and nearer to a restored human integrity, the more it is conformed to the divine.

We have already seen, speaking quite practically, that priests are inhibited in their effectiveness by the way their separation is perceived. This is the common experience of many English clergy, to look no further. The image of the stage curate, the harmless nitwit who preserves the vision of innocence in a guilty world, makes the priest a good mascot but useless when real agony has to be faced. But it is just there, when the priest is drawn into the distress of others, that the paradox can be resolved and priesthood find its own validity. If a suffering person can see that the priest sent to him by God is no stranger to his suffering, and is actually able to enter into it and speak for it as truthfully as he does himself, then he can find a resource in that priest which is both human and from God. It is at such moments that we can see some sense in the idea that consecration to God has to make people more and not less human, more open to the needs and feelings and struggles of humanity. The separation of priests stands not in their removal from humanity but in the universal quality which God gives to their humanity.

Now, this universality is not a matter of regular experience. It does not lie to hand. It has to be sought by responsible discipline, as a goal that informs all the particular tendencies of priests' lives. They have to see that they are given their experience of humanity, not only in order to make something of it for themselves, but in order to make something of it for all. And, beyond the quest and discipline, the universality the priest seeks has to be received as a gift. That is the special significance of those moments when a priest finds he or she can stand beside people in God's name, and share with them in the discovery of the liberty God gives.

It is not remarkable then that the Epistle to the Hebrews finds the one essential positive human character of priesthood in the quality of compassion (Heb. 2.17 & 18; 3.15 & 16). To become a true priest Jesus has to be faithful and compassionate and that in turn demands that he should not stand apart from humankind but become entirely one with it. Abstract concepts of divinity can only serve the division of God from humankind, but the active compassionate love of God unites him to men and women. Priesthood is possible in love.

But that of course does nothing to make priesthood valid as a general institution, nor does it do anything to relieve the individual priest's sense that their task is beyond them. Strictly speaking it is beyond them. Its performance does not lie within their grasp. If love is the answer, who can match the love of God in his or her own actions?

5. Christ, the Fulfilment of Priesthood

For the Christian tradition, the idea of priesthood finds its fulfilment and vindication in Christ. It is in Jesus that the necessity of priesthood is satisfied and its impossibility overcome. In his human life God's relation to humankind is fully articulated, not tentatively or in a compromised way but with an adequacy that cannot be surpassed. The fear of idolatry is taken away. As we have seen, we become apprehensive about idolatry when we perceive that religion is something we devise, in which our personal interests are bound up. Jesus strips himself of all such interests, and rather than devise a programme for himself, gives himself up to the will of the one he calls Father. Jesus does not take priesthood upon himself (and there is the impossibility of priesthood, for us, in a single phrase. We take it for ourselves all the time!) but he is called to it, 'as Aaron was, by God' (Heb. 5.4). Jesus, the Christ, then, is seen as the one in whom self-assertiveness in both its personal and social forms is overcome and who is filled with the compassion that alone establishes priesthood as real.

He is a true priest also, not only in the quality of his priesthood but in the fullness of its scope. In various theological traditions Jesus is believed to hold three offices, of prophet, priest and king. That is to say that he unites in himself the three sacral ministries which had been most typical of Israel and whose diversity shows what priesthood is about more fully than any of them alone. The choice of the three titles is, of course, shaped by biblical tradition. These are, so to speak, the three callings which God has willed to be found in human society for his own sake as well as ours. Each is a way in which God is represented among men and women. But though the terminology is Israelite, the experiences are universal. Wherever societies develop and diversify, sacral offices tend to diversify as well. And as in Israel, so elsewhere, diverse offices are always signs of potential division in human life and faith. The process of mediation between God and humankind is fragmented. It is like a sentence which ought to state clearly how God and humanity stand in relation to one another, but which has been divided into clauses that no longer fit together. Here too we meet the impossibility of priesthood. In its purpose, priesthood touches everything and unites everything in the name of God's universal concern. In practice, different aspects of life and faith break away from the whole. If Jesus is really prophet, priest and king he has reconciled in himself what in history has always tended to division.

Society as a whole ought to acknowledge God in its daily life, but this demands an appropriate institutional structure, and so far no single institution has ever proved sufficient. The ideal priesthood attributed to Christ is conceived by a projection from our experience of diverse unfulfilled and partial attempts to provide such a structure – an attempt to describe something which gathers up and unites them all.[6] Prophecy, priesthood, kingship all show us something of how it is between God and us, but the range of each is restricted. The competition between them, and the way in which, in this fragmented state, institutions have always proved more deadly than liberating, show that we need something beyond what we have seen so far. Christ's threefold office can be seen as a promise that this 'something beyond' is attainable and worth striving for.

Kingship is undoubtedly a sacral office. Only in a completely secularised culture could we find a Head of State who was acknowledged to emerge by mere human choice, and to serve merely functional purposes. In practice such an office is hard to find. The rituals of kingship are still carried out, in one form or another, even when their meaning is consciously denied. Anciently a king was recognised as the bearer of sacred meaning for his people, an image of God, a sign that God and people stood in some kind of established relationship. The political nature of the office did not prevent it being also in some sense priestly. Indeed, the office carried a firm conviction that politics is not separable from the reign of God, that worship and civic life are meant to be in harmony with one another. Such an idea undoubtedly has its sinister side. It could mean the subordination of worship to political interests, as religious symbolism is called in to give support to arrogance, or to cover up incompetence. The alliance of political and religious power is always a threat to human values.

Nevertheless, this is to draw out only one side of a complex position, and the one most obvious in the modern world. We know that religion can be used as a form of mystification – a way in which ruling interests seize upon powerful and well-seeming images to hide the reality of their tyranny from others or even themselves. But this is only half the story. Only if the king is held to represent God without being accountable to God is this cynical interpretation true to the institution itself. In fact a king *can* be held to account, as the story of David and Bathsheba in the Old Testament shows, or the story of Creon and Antigone in the Greek tradition. And if the king *is* accountable, the whole people can be made accountable to God through him.[7]

But this is again an ideal, and an incomplete ideal at that. In practice politics and religion are in tension with one another. The tension is felt at state level, where rulers and church leaders jostle with one another uneasily, and it is felt by ordinary lay people who are never sure how to reconcile their secular life with religion. The simplest way to contain this tension is to build up separate institutions to represent the two poles. As in Israel, kings can develop their power in a secular direction, and leave it to a distinct priesthood to exercise religious authority. Or they can relinquish political power to more pragmatic organs of state, as happened in republican Rome and Athens and again in our own society, and then dwindle into politically insignificant cultic personages. Either way, we see, the idea that God can really be served in political society is too big to swallow whole. It has to be broken into pieces. Kings and priests move apart, and (to take the case of Israel, or mediaeval Europe as typical) though the king may be given religious legitimation he does not claim to represent God directly. He can immerse himself in the brutalities and squalors of *raison d'état* without compromising the religious symbols that originally secured his kingship. Priesthood, on the other hand, becomes the custodian of these symbols, in which the transcendence of the sacred remains uncompromised though only at the cost of disengagement from practical matters. The union of kingship and priesthood in one person, or even one system, can be seen as a sign that in principle the whole of society is capable of consecration to God. Separation between the offices, and the divergence of rulers from priests, can be seen as a token that this principle has lost its force in society. The consecration of the life of humankind is known only in a compromised and frustrated condition. Its fulfilment must wait for another day. But to say that Christ is both king and priest is to say that, however proleptically, that day has come.

Now kingship and priesthood are both institutional ways in which the orientation of a society toward God can be expressed. But there is another aspect of human fellowship with God which has to be acknowledged, and which often fits badly with both of them. This is the element often called *charismatic*, that impulse toward spontaneity in religion which ranges beyond institutions and often threatens to break them. Here the knowledge of God is looked for, not only in public symbols but also (or in extreme cases exclusively) within the soul, in personal fellowship, in the communion of spirit with spirits, in visions and dreams and miracles and in other unpredictable events. In Israel it was peculiarly the prophets who carried this note – men and women laid under special obligation to God so that their personalities, their very hearts, were given up to be vehicles of God's word. The prophet who can say, 'This is the Word of the Lord', has to set aside any fear of established authority. The word he or she has been given puts everything in question – his or her own complacency and self-protectiveness along with that of everyone else.

All religion has to find room for something of this kind to happen, or, if God is represented only in official rites and formulas, he is as much bound to them as his priests and people are, and is really shown to be no God at all. That is why, although the charismatic element is always awkward to get on with, institutional religion seldom tries to drive it out altogether. It may try to regulate it, above all to interpret it, but in the end it cannot do without it. In some sense, God really is what charismatic religion represents him to be, sovereign and free to question all that we have established in his name. The institution needs to feel the impact of unfettered charism as a check on its own tendency to restrain God and cut him down to its own size.

At the same time charismatic religion needs to be linked with tradition and institution if it is not to dissipate itself in undirected feeling. There is no experience more dangerous in the spiritual life than an intuitive experience that goes beyond all reason. Unless the event is interpreted and helped to become fruitful in a tradition of life, the effect of such an experience may easily be personal dissolution and the loss of all reality. The prophets, though their social critique is radical, make sure that they criticise real society for real faults, and they draw upon the institutional traditions of Israel's calling to validate what they say. Priesthood and prophecy, institution and charism, need one another if God is to be served in the historical life of mankind.

So, when it is said that Jesus is prophet, priest and king, we are to see the force of this, not in the accumulation of separate offices, but in their reconciliation and union. Jesus represents the possibility of drawing together, in a new integrity, all the separate modes of relating us to God. Form and spontaneity work together, outward institution and inner motive, God in his faithfulness and God in his surprising inventiveness. And all this, not in 'mere' religion, but in complete union with the whole of human concern. Faith and politics become a field of common endeavour, the individual love of God with the common life of society. The social necessity of priesthood finds its fulfilment here without triumphing over the liberty of the Spirit, or the dexterity of divine wisdom.

This vision of the service of God made one and whole again is especially pertinent to our own times. In modern western society religious impulses appear in many guises, incompatible with one another and stultifying in themselves. Priesthood and cult have not been abolished but they easily become divorced from everything else and lapse into social sterility. Politicians assert the freedom of politics from religious restraint but also try to harness religious-sounding rhetoric to political ends. And, between the two, many individuals try to escape from the dilemmas of social existence by cultivating private religious feelings. The knowledge of God is fragmented, and the fragments are turned against one another. The union of priesthood with prophecy and kingship in Jesus speaks of a wholeness that we badly need and rebukes our despair at failing to achieve it.

Yet the way in which Jesus has attained to the state of wholeness only confirms the conviction that, in this world and short of the ultimate reconciliation of all things with God, priesthood is impossible. For Jesus comes to the fullness of his office, only by way of death. So far as the New Testament encourages us to call Jesus prophet, priest, or king, it reminds us at the same time that these terms fit him only as one condemned to crucifixion. He is the prophet who must perish in Jerusalem (Luke 13.33). He is named a high priest, only when he has learned obedience through the things that he suffered (Heb. 5.8 & 9). He is a king, whose kingly title is published on the cross itself (John 19.19–22). Jesus enters into the fullness to which these sacral titles point only by a radical disengagement from the present order of the world through death. And even if we reply that he is glorified and that his Spirit lives and works in the church, we have to see that the resurrection and the Spirit point us back to the cross as the place where God has made himself known. God has articulated his presence in the midst of humankind in the only way that takes account of our inarticulateness. The inarticulateness itself remains. All that can be said of the necessity of priesthood, and of its impossibility, is summed up in the cross.

Then, if that is the way God's truth is expressed, how can such a truth take on a social form and communicate itself to us? What kind of tradition, what kind of priesthood, must the death of God's own Son give rise to?

CHAPTER TWO

The Universal Moment – Priesthood and Ministry in the New Testament

And every moment is a new and shocking
Valuation of all we have been
T. S. Eliot, *East Coker*

1. The Gospel as Re-evaluation

If the institutions that human society devises, in order to relate itself to the sacred, point to a certain fulfilment, an ideal state of existence, they also contribute to a heightened sense of unfulfilment. The high claims that have to be made for sacral institutions are never finally substantiated. More often than not, priests are disappointing creatures, and if in practice men and women are still not disappointed it is as much because they are determined not to be as because they are fully satisfied. Secretly or openly, a concern for priesthood is an exercise in hope. Something better is always being sought.

The gospel of Christ is at least a declaration that something better has come. The gospel, as witnessed to throughout the New Testament, speaks of a changed awareness on the part of humankind in its relation to God. God has declared himself in Christ to be a God of grace, of mercy and of love. He takes away the guilt of those who turn to him. He draws them to himself in a spirit of liberty. They come to him, not as slaves but as sons and daughters. The more radically this change of awareness is grasped, the more clear it is that every sentiment and conviction that has informed the religion of the past is under judgement, and that the institutional structures that have sustained these sentiments are now being severely questioned. If God is a God of grace, the ministries that are undertaken in his name cannot be the same as they would be for a merely natural or cultural god, still less a god of caprice, of wrath or of strict and equal justice. And while we must agree that God as acknowledged in Judaism is none of these things, nevertheless, the radical thrust of the new perceptions must at least call the forms of acknowledgement to account.

If we are to discuss the way the New Testament authors handle such subjects as priesthood, office and structure in the church, it is here we must start, with the radical questioning of deep-rooted institutional necessities. Christians have come to turn to the New Testament, in a way that is almost wearisomely automatic, for texts about ministry, in the hope that they will find there something secure and relevant to their own needs. They have assumed that if an institutional structure is to be found in the church at all it will receive its legitimacy from something clearly directed to that end in the Bible. At least the foundations of the future edifice will have been laid in the first century and witnessed to in scripture. And the search for positive validation can have a negative effect as well. 'We do not find this in scripture!' It may be that no foundations are evident, no structure is legitimated, because, to put it crudely, God does not intend such things for the church.

Those who take either view find the actual terrain of scripture difficult to ride. Something always lies in the way of a consistent path. Always there appears a piece of contrary evidence. It is certainly not easy to discern continuity between the New Testament church and the institutional form of the church in later centuries, but neither does the New Testament give support to a bland unconcern for Christian institutions. This elusive quality in the New Testament witness arises from the nature of the earliest Christian experience itself. The earliest Christians were not consciously laying foundations, but neither were they set on destroying them. They were caught up in a process of radical reappraisal of all that belongs to religion, in such a way that the nature of what was being questioned and the question itself were repeatedly being perceived afresh.

The New Testament is not the record of a single consistent perception, nor of a process of discovery pursued in one direction only. Rather it speaks of a process like growing up, in which children who are no longer quite children have to learn again and again what it means to be an adult, having so far only the experience of a child to help them judge. New strengths, new liberties, new modes of recognition by their neighbours are given them, but because these things have not been proved and tested, the young person who has been made aware of them is often left feeling weaker and more desolate than ever before. The one thing you must not ask of people struggling into maturity is a consistent account of themselves.

A young bird is born with wings, but it does not use them to fly. Even when it is fledged it will find other uses for them first. A young shearwater uses them as paddles to help out its almost useless legs. A young thrush in a tree will use them to steady itself as it hops from branch to branch. Only later comes a moment when the young bird has to take its weight off its feet, trust to the air and fly. That is the moment when it really discovers its wings.

Such a moment came to Christians in the earliest church when they learned to enter fully into the faith they had already confessed. It is one thing to know that Jesus is Lord when the earth seems stable, and another to know it when all the familiar safeguards are falling away. It is one thing to see that a gospel of grace modifies the way people stand before God within a system of law, and another to perceive that the system itself is made incoherent by the principle of grace. In such a moment all the old constraints, which were also assurances, have to be re-examined. Faith, in that situation, invites and compels people to see that they *can* undertake this reassessment. They do not have to be afraid. Even though the secure ground has fallen away beneath them, they are supported, and supported in an infinitely more exciting enviroment.

It is this moment which I want to call *the universal moment* – the moment when particular guarantees and requirements crumble, and the whole of existence has to be re-appropriated in a new way. At that moment I may have lost all sense of how I coped in the past, or will order my affairs for the future, but I know who I am.

2. The Nature of the New Testament Witness

We can take hold of this moment historically and sociologically by considering the way the earliest churches developed in relation to the world of their time. The earliest attempts at Christian common life took place within the social context of Judaism. Christianity was, in the eyes of others and in its own eyes, a variant in the already varied pattern of Jewish culture. Nevertheless this position could not be sustained. The gospel itself, declaring that the crucified Jesus was in fact the fulfiller of Jewish hopes, was too much for many Jews to accept. The Christian movement had had its origin in a certain antagonism between Jesus himself and the rulers of the Jewish nation – an antagonism that was never healed at the official level. And then, when the church opened its life toward the Gentiles, it came to face questions that its predominantly Jewish ideas could not answer, and no obvious home became available to it in the Gentile world either. The state would not recognise it. The sophisticated or philosophically-minded were inclined to despise it, and a Christian's pagan neighbour was morally and religiously offended by his new pattern of behaviour. The church was forced into a non-institutional existence, outside all law, recognised by no convention, no prince, no priest. The common life of Christians, in spite of its vitality, had to find its place in the interstices of official society, with no secure arrangement about where it really belonged. Not surprisingly, the Christians were perplexed about this. If some, like the Johannine community, turned inward, ostensibly upon the God who gave himself only as an inward gift, others like Paul continued to look for God's presence and for opportunities to serve him outside the ecclesiastical circle, though with an uneasy sense of moral danger (1 Cor. 10.27).

There were different responses to the situation, then, for the universal moment came to different individuals and Christian groups in different ways. A Jewish Christian congregation might have to break with the synagogue and live its own life. A Christian man with a public position might suffer the loss of reputation for the sake of Christ. 'My grace is sufficient for you,' had to be learned afresh by people who had been speaking confidently of Christ's grace all along. For the universal moment is a moment of transition from a closed world to an open one, from a world in which God is present only in the supporting and constraining structures to one in which he stands above them and strives to win us from reliance upon them. However it came upon them it would make Christians feel themselves to be strangers in the world, and to appear strangers to their fellows.

The most fully documented and personally attested example of this is to be found in Paul's struggle to relate himself afresh to the Jewish Law, the Torah, which had provided the total context of his life up to the time of his conversion. Paul insists upon a 'righteousness of God revealed apart from the Law' – a righteousness available to the uncircumcised and the ungodly (Rom. 3.21, 30; 4.5) – because he is so firmly convinced that the grace of God alone can provide the basis of a truly human life. And yet even he wants this same Law, which he has virtually defined as graceless, to testify to its own supersession by the gospel. (Rom. 3.21) The divine transcendence of institutions still needs its institutional attestation. There can be no consistency here. Paul simply holds to what he knows, even if he cannot reconcile its several parts.[1]

The same tension appears in John's gospel, in the contrast drawn between Moses and Jesus (1.17; 9.28), between the Jews and the disciples (9.22), between the approval of men and the approval of God (5.44, 12.43) – as severe a separation as the New Testament witnesses to – yet informed by the contrary conviction that Jesus fulfils the Old Testament scriptures (5.39), and that he belongs among the Jews (4.22).

But the same struggle between new and old, grace and institution, could be illustrated without breaking through the Jewish perimeter. In the synoptic gospels Jesus upsets people's sense of social order by his proclamation that the kingdom is given to the publicans and harlots (Matt. 21.31), to the poor (Luke 6.20) and to the sinful (Matt. 9.13), while in the Epistle of James there is a surprisingly fierce denunciation of religious cant and common prudence, and a call to a fresh, invigorating trust in God (1.22ff, 2.16, 4.15). What is common to these traces of the universal moment is not their terminology, their social context, or even the kind of behaviour they point to, but the sense in each of them that nothing upon which we have come to rely is an adequate vehicle for the saving presence of God. God always points away and beyond. When he acts, he does so simply in his own person.

But it is also true that the New Testament bears witness to the passing of this moment. Grace has to be converted into habit. A 'man in Christ' is allowed to know himself as such, and in that sense label himself once more. It is in the New Testament itself that we can trace the first attempts of the church to apprehend itself institutionally. The heady struggles for Christian freedom that we find in Galatians and Romans are notoriously out of key with the desire we find in the Pastoral Epistles to maintain tradition and to guarantee sound teaching. Yet both represent moments in the church's struggle to discover itself under God. The Pastorals' concern for sobriety is less exhilarating than the fervours of *sola gratia*, but Paul himself was aware that vertiginous enthusiasm is not the best condition for a godly life in community (1 Cor. 12.2;

14.40). The problem is never at any time, 'whether?' order is appropriate but, 'what?'. Nevertheless the universal moment is truly universal. Christians enter it again and again, as individuals or as churches, in every age and in all kinds of circumstances. For again and again we are challenged to see that the arrangements we have made, and the formulas we have adopted in our response to God's grace, are not adequate for it. Grace overflows the containers we provide, and bursts out beyond the limits we suppose to be appropriate.

The New Testament, we can say, hands on to the church of later times a double witness and a double task. On the one hand it can be seen as itself an attempt to articulate the gospel and to give discernible form to the Christian's awareness that God has acted decisively on his or her behalf. It is indeed the product of Christian attempts to articulate the gospel during the period when its challenge was new and the saving events were still a matter of direct experience. But on the other hand it witnesses to the impossibility of articulating that gospel in any permanently sufficient form. It points away from the structures that claim divine institution and insists upon God himself as the source of every saving grace and the object of saving faith (2 Cor. 1.9). So it lays upon us the duty to speak intelligibly (1 Cor. 14.15), and also to be silent ('that every mouth may be stopped,' Rom. 3.19), to plan and to work, and also to wait for the dissolution of all that we have done (1 Cor. 7.29–31).

This double-sidedness of the New Testament message makes any reference to its authority highly dangerous. It is not that it has no authority, but we cannot calculate beforehand what it will authorise us to do. As the original witness to God's saving acts, performed in his own person, it is bound to enter into every fresh attempt to testify to those acts. All subsequent Christian speech and writing is essentially commentary upon these scriptures, worked out in dialogue with them, dependent upon them and derivative from them. But even the New Testament cannot be taken as a final institutional codification of authority in the church, in the face of the insistence so often made within it that no such institution can exist. Those who speak to us through the New Testament speak as witnesses who want us to perceive, in the end, not themselves but God. They offer to share their perception with us, but they impose no solutions and they require no submission.

Teachers can be divided broadly into two kinds. There are those who handle their subject systematically, and who enable their pupils to do the same, at least within the bounds of the system they have expounded. But there are those whose approach is more critical, occasional and fragmentary. They show what others have said and done, to expose their insights and also their limitations. They stimulate their pupils to offer answers to questions, and then help them transcend and so criticise the answers they have arrived at. They show that learning is largely a matter of living with questions and not abandoning the freedom to do so. Such teaching cannot itself be systematised, except perhaps in a few pregnant aphorisms, and it is a betrayal of such teaching when the demolishers of authority are themselves set up as authorities and expected to lend their names to ready-made answers.

We betray the witness of the New Testament when we make it an authority of this restricting kind. The primary activity of the New Testament is to witness to Jesus, and, in his name, to question and criticise every human position in relation to God. In this way it presses us toward that moment when we let go of our human security sufficiently to trust in the living God as one who loves us now. The slogan *sola scriptura*, the Bible alone, is a good one if it stands for the recognition that ultimately men and women cannot work out their own standing with God for themselves. They must allow themselves to be addressed, judged and set free. But if *sola scriptura* is taken to mean that the scripture itself is a final authority, requiring an imitative conformity or an exclusive assent, it becomes a slogan that transgresses the nature of the scriptural message itself. It seeks answers in the place where God has put questions, and sets obedience to a rule above Christ's gift of freedom to explore.

3. The Content of the New Testament Witness

How then are we to approach those passages in the New Testament which speak of the mutual service of Christians, or of the Christian's engagement with others in Christ's name, or which deal with ecclesiastical office, or which employ the language of priesthood? We are not to treat them as stereotypes, or as legitimating precedents. Rather we are to consider them in their dynamism, and prepare to enter into that dynamism ourselves. The key ideas of the New Testament seize us because they have transformative potential. They take closed situations and break them open, not nihilistically but hopefully. Their essential power is that of Christ's death and resurrection which shatters an old world only to point forward into a new one. They encourage us to take up the task of New Testament Christianity, even though in times which are quite different and therefore in quite different ways, because we are still held by the same promise of faith.

The earliest churches were not primarily concerned with words, or with the ideas that words convey. They called upon the power of language to serve a common life of service and worship, and to give direction to practical concerns. The 'word', for them, was essentially God's personal speech to mankind. God's grace was offered, not to be recorded or analysed, but as a call to repentance and faith, and so to practical response. The New Testament is through and through occasional. All its writings are directed to particular situations, and have to be read as prompting Christians to certain ways of living and as warning them against others, rather than as explorations of ideas for their own sake.

If then we ask why New Testament writers sometimes use sacral language, the language of priesthood, sacrifice and temple, we must look for the answer in something more than a mere fascination with sacral imagery. When Christ's death is described as a sacrifice (Eph. 5.2), or Christians in their solidarity are called a priesthood (1 Pet. 2.9), these are not just illuminating metaphors for things which are really not sacral at all. These things are said, not to make an intellectual comparison but to stake a claim. The Christians of New Testament times lived in societies that were thoroughly moulded at the root of their instincts by sacral institutions. Priesthood, temple and cultus were not just ornaments of social existence; they were perceived as essential to the social fabric. So when Christians turned to this kind of language they were not trying merely to illuminate the belief of their hearts. They were also interpreting their social position.

Now, according to all the usual measures, that social position was increasingly weak. Christ had been excluded from society, both physically and morally, by his condemnation and crucifixion. Christians were to turn again and again to that exclusion as the key to their own exclusion from the esteem and security that comes through social recognition. Like Christ they were called to suffer, and, like him, 'outside the camp' (Heb. 13.11–13). That did not mean, however, that in their own, or as they saw it, in God's understanding they were weak, discredited and insecure. On the contrary, it was their common standing with Christ in the face of society's derision that constituted their true strength, credit, and security. Compared with what God had established for them by the death and resurrection of Christ, no merely human judgement could count, even that of the weightiest human authorities.

So in the matter of priesthood, sacrifice and temple, it should not surprise us that the earliest Christians were led to claim that it was they, and not the society that excluded them, who possessed the true substance (Heb. 10.1; 11.1) of these things. Although the Christian common life was lacking in anything resembling an institutional priesthood, or a temple made with hands, or a plainly cultic offering, the claim could be made that it was Christians and not others who knew the reality of temple, priesthood and sacrifice. That meant in turn that a more genuine social sensibility was at work in them than in others, and that it was the gospel of Christ and not the myths and cultural prejudices of mankind that offered a basis for true society.

The claim is made most plainly, though with some idiosyncrasy, in the Epistle to the Hebrews. It is made, characteristically, not for Christians but for Christ. He it is who substantiates priesthood and sacrifice, while the social institutions that are supposed to represent these things do so only in figure, as shadows of the heavenly and spiritual reality which is attained to in Jesus (Heb. 9.23–10.7). According to the epistle's author, Jewish priesthood and the sacrifices instituted by the Law are insufficient to accomplish the end they seem to promise. They cannot truly secure the remission of sins, they cannot really offer free access to God. But Jesus, through his obedience, suffering and death, has been offered as a sacrifice and established as a priest in a complete and final way. Effective mediation between God and humanity lies with him, and everything else that expresses mediation is but an insubstantial copy.

Now it is obvious that language is here being stretched in a bold, not to say bizarre, way. Yet in the author's mind, and for anyone who takes his point, this extension of language is not to be seen as a transplanting of ideas from their natural place to one less natural, but as a coming home. We have not any kind of metaphor here. For the author, the proper application of this language is to Jesus, and to the experience of Jesus which Christians are able to share. That is where it is used 'naturally' according to the nature of things as God has constituted them. Jesus is the real and permanent embodiment of the meaning of priesthood. Those who have faith in him are not metaphorically saved, sanctified, and brought to God, but really, fully and finally. And since, for the author, all dealing with God depends on the reality of priesthood, the standing of Christians before God can only be grounded in Christ's own real, though spiritual and heavenly, priesthood.

Behind the argument of Hebrews there is an exact sense of the nature of analogy. We sometimes speak of metaphor and analogy as the same thing. When people say, 'this is metaphor or analogy', they do not normally mean, 'either one or the other, I'm not sure which', but, 'that kind of thing, call it whatever you like'. Alas for distinctions! we could do with more, and here they are essential. Metaphor and analogy are alike in being examples of extended language, but they can also be vigorously contrasted.[2]

Metaphors are the once-for-all coinages of imaginative speech. They are the sudden revisions of convention that are demanded by new perceptions, and which retain their currency only while the perception remains new. Metaphors are precipitated when one particular situation is perceived in an original way, in terms of another. And part of their effect depends upon our ability to see the two situations separately, in plain terms, and at the same time enjoy their conjunction. Metaphors serve understanding, but even more, they serve delight, and the delight lies, at least in part, in seeing two familiar images unite in something never seen before. When Keats writes, 'O for a beaker full of the warm south!' we can picture to ourselves both the glass of wine he would like to pour out for himself, all in its matter-of-factness, and also the charm of a Mediterranean summer that he associates with it – which for him is integral with it. Metaphor works by making us see the association as integral, and so illuminates for us what would otherwise be ordinary and unmemorable. Every time a metaphor works it does so through the particularity of the associations it invokes. Ideally every metaphor is a unique ocurrence in the world of language, a conjunction of ideas that only on this occasion can exert the peculiar influence it does.

When metaphors are repeated they either develop into analogy or decline and die. Dead metaphors are found when the original perception has been tamed and use of the image has become habitual.[3] The conjunction ceases to illuminate and the words used, though figurative still, are no more than a slangy substitute for the plain expression that might have been used. Here we suffer the loss of meaning rather than its gain.

Analogy works quite differently. Analogy is the trace, within human language, of our dealings with mystery. We resort to analogy, not to illuminate a reality that would otherwise be plain, but one that would otherwise be dark. We use analogous speech because plain speech is not available. We work from familiar experience, and the words appropriate to it, to something which could never be familiar, however strong and persistent its impact upon us. In the process the meaning of the words we use is stretched, it is true, and grammar and logic break down. And yet we sense that the mystery we are concerned with means more to us, and has a better title to the language we use, than the familiar situation in which dull people would say it properly belongs. God is described in language drawn from our experience of created perfection, but it appertains to him with more certainty than it does to creatures.[4] It is not at all that perfection belongs to his creatures and he imitates it, but that perfection belongs to him, and his creatures only participate in it by his gift.

So when Hebrews claims that Jesus is a true priest it is not claiming that Jesus is a priest in the bodily and temporal way that the priests of historical Israel were. However, to exclude that part of the word's connotation is not to diminish its meaning, but to enhance it. To say that Jesus is eternally a priest, in a spiritual and heavenly way, is to say that he is a priest indeed (Heb. 7.16).

It would be wrong then to suppose that when the New Testament authors in general use this image of priesthood to articulate Christian experience they are using it with attenuated force. Hebrews, it is true, is the only example in the New Testament of a sustained and systematic use of this language, designed to set out a deliberate comparison between Christian and Jewish experiences and priesthood. Other uses of the imagery, abundant as they are, do have the quality of metaphor in that they are used on occasion, aimed at a single illumination in the course of an argument, and often in combination with quite different kinds of terminology. Nevertheless the frequency with which this figurative sacral language is used, and the way in which the several uses establish a kind of consistency among themselves, suggest that we are not dealing here with unstructured happy illuminations. Either these metaphors are growing sick through repetition and are near to death, or we are reckoning with an intuition that must have been widely shared in the church, that this language pointed to something substantial in Christian experience, however difficult it might be to grasp.

One sign of this is that the language has doctrinal force, and that there is something to be conveyed through it that admits no other expression. Another is that even as a figure of speech this language can be elaborated. Metaphors are not merely coined and spent. They are developed in a manner comparable with that of the metaphysical poets, into conceits. Consider, for example the two much-quoted verses from 1 Peter.

> 'You also, as living stones, are built up a spiritual house, to be a holy priesthood, to offer spiritual sacrifices acceptable to God through Jesus Christ.' (1 Pet. 2.5)
>
> 'But you are an elect race, a royal priesthood, a holy nation, a people for God's own possession, that you may show forth the excellencies of him who called you out of darkness into his own marvellous light.' (1 Pet. 2.9)

The basic comparison here is with the Old Testament concept of Israel as (in God's intention) a holy nation (Exod. 19.5 & 6). It is sometimes explained that the force of the words 'royal priesthood' is to claim a special status for Christians – the status of a people set apart for God. Yet, in fact, the words go beyond status (though they include it) and speak of action as well. Christians are to proclaim the mighty works of God and to offer spiritual sacrifices, and though none of this means that they seek to fulfil the social function of the socially instituted priesthoods it does suggest that the idea of priesthood in the church is capable of systematic development.

Again, Paul in Romans 15.16 describes himself as 'a minister of Christ Jesus unto the Gentiles, ministering the gospel of God, that the offering of the Gentiles might be acceptable, being sanctified by the Holy Spirit.' Here every expression used, except the word *gospel* and the names of God, Christ and the Spirit are cultic and sacrificial terms. It needs only a fanciful rhyme scheme to make the comparison with the metaphysicals complete. Paul has brought together several distinct references to experience in one comprehensive organising metaphor – his own preaching, the response of the hearers, the content of the gospel, the action of the Spirit, and the relationship between God and the peoples of the world. The end of Paul's ministry is not only worship, but worship which he is not ashamed to describe in the technical language of worship. Paul's use of sacrificial imagery here is too fully thought out for us to say that it just offered itself to him on this occasion. It is only shortly before in Romans that he sums up the moral response of Christians to God's grace as 'the offering of your bodies as a living sacrifice, your reasonable worship' (Rom. 12.1). Beneath these occasional uses there is, it seems, some fundamental perception of the congruence between Christian life and sacrificial imagery. New Testament Christianity has a priestly consciousness of itself, which draws it back repeatedly to priestly ideas to describe its concerns and its activities. At the same time it is important to note that no attempt is made in the New Testament itself to give this consciousness systematic expression except in Hebrews.

To attempt a synthesis of these things would therefore be to go well beyond what is actually said in the Bible. Where syntheses are produced we can call them constructive and apologetic attempts at a Christian theology of priesthood, and there is nothing wrong with such things in principle, but they are not biblical theology. What can be attempted within the bounds of biblical study is to discern what it is in Christian consciousness that lies below the varied and unsystematic use of priestly and cultic language in the New Testament. The fundamental idea seems to be that the cultic institutions which appear in society are a figure, either of the total action of Christ as revealed in his death, or the total moral life of Christians, which is also of course grounded in Christ crucified and risen. Cultic action has become one with the whole of human action so far as it is turned towards God. This is not to 'spiritualise' the idea, in the sense of making it over to some unseen world, nor does it reduce it to merely mental notions and dispositions of the heart, for the consecration of the heart and the 'renewal of the mind' (Rom. 12.2) inevitably lead to characteristic action. It is this *action* which is conceived to be priestly or sacrificial. Jesus really does commit himself to death on the cross, and that (rather than any bare intention) is his sacrifice. Paul really does proclaim the gospel committed to him, and that is his 'liturgy', what makes him a *leitourgos* (Rom. 15.16). The 'living sacrifice' of Romans 12 is worked out in acts of mutual service, and it is only through these things that the bodies of Christians are really made over to God in sacrifice.

The effect of these uses, then, is not so much to turn the sacral imagery inward, as to set it free from particular institutions and to make it universal. The limitations that social arrangements impose upon the exercise of priesthood are here, at least in principle, dissolved. Priesthood becomes – and it is tempting to say, becomes afresh – the calling and activity of every human being. It is as though all the New Testament ideas about priesthood are rooted in an inchoate but vivid intuition of natural and universal human priesthood – a potential priesthood of every man and woman.

It must be clear of course that this 'priesthood of humanity'[5] does not imply a right or claim to office in society. Quite the contrary. Compared with the priesthood of humanity – a priesthood that is exercised through common prayer and worship, through neighbourly acts, through repentance and love and the confession of God's goodness – the institutional priesthoods which society develops have to be seen as an admission of failure. It is as though the consecration of human life has to be acted out in show because it is not achieved in reality. If that is so, then the various references in the New Testament to priesthood can be read as claims to the restoration of that reality through the work of Christ.

At this point we may well ask, what is the link between this Christian perception of a universal human priesthood, and the elements of priesthood which, we suggested in chapter 1, are diffused throughout all social experience. The answer is that they are not the same, but that the one assumes the other. In our rudimentary priestly acts we offer people an account of themselves by which they can locate themselves in life. The Christian perception of a universal priesthood testifies that the only true account of that kind is one that lays people's lives open to God. What they have in common is a readiness not only to face the question of human meaning but to give it an answer.

Hebrews takes up from Psalm 8 the question, 'What is man?' and answers it by reference to the humiliation and exaltation of Jesus (Heb. 2.6–9). For Hebrews, it seems, full humanity exists only in Jesus, and so real priesthood is to be found only in him as well. Paul and 1 Peter complement the narrow focus of Hebrews on Jesus by the way they see 'humanity restored in Christ' and 'priesthood restored in Christ' as corporate modes of existence in which the whole church, and by intention, the whole of humankind can share. The church's corporate priestliness separates it from the rest of humankind, only in the way that those who anticipate the future and lay claim to its promise are separated from those who remain, as yet, shut up in the past. But when Paul speaks of the offering of the Gentiles being made acceptable to God he implies that the spiritual worship of the Gentiles does not wait upon the gospel for its existence but only for its release. The Gentiles already have something – their bodies, their very selves – to offer God, and God is already open to that offering, but the work of the Holy Spirit in the preaching of the gospel is needed to consecrate that offering, to make it effective.

These are the possibilities that open themselves to human vision in the universal moment, the moment when we find ourselves in the hands of God without the support of institutions. New Testament Christians were free to explore, to widen and to reapply the concept of priesthood in this way because they were not tied to a restricted priesthood of their own which had to be upheld, explained and rationalised. Because they had been forced to let go of priesthood as a social structure they were able to rediscover the fullness of priesthood in Christ. In the process the idea of priesthood was both widened in the scope of its application and deepened in meaning. As we have seen already, the compassion of Christ was seen in Hebrews as the distinctive test of the reality of his priesthood, and more generally, his 'cultic' work is seen as inseparable from his love. Now who could deny, even among the ministers of the church, that institutions of themselves tend to inhibit the working of love, and to threaten the unity of priest and people. Perhaps the renewal of priesthood in New Testament experience is nowhere so evident as here, that the idea of priesthood has been recovered to mean the liberation of compassion and the fulfilment of love.

With that in mind we should now return to the observation that in the New Testament there is also a movement toward the institutionalisation of the church. There is a developing recognition of Christian sacraments, Christian scriptures, and of ministerial office and structure. Paul, who in some of his arguments is as distrustful of religious institutions as the most broadminded liberal, also shows a readiness to insist on faithfulness to certain traditional Christian practices (1 Cor. 11.16). He denounces reliance on circumcision (Gal. 5.2), but is prepared to base a crucial argument in Romans on the universality of Baptism (Rom. 6.1–11), while in another place he tries to get the Corinthian Christians to see that the Lord's Supper is a better alternative to the sacrificial meals they once shared in as pagans (1 Cor. 10.21).

In one way, this simply marks the fact that the church was persisting through time and was aware of itself as doing so. It is not difficult to live without clearly defined institutions when you believe that all institutions are soon to be swept away in any case. Apocalyptic fervour and a certain carelessness about the church's identity over time often go together. What tends to matter where this spirit dominates is the cohesion of this group here and now. When, in the New Testament, we find that institutional forms are being recognised in the church, we can see this as a sign that the church is becoming more aware of itself as a social and institutional group. The identity of this group demands some kind of enduring expression. The Christian Church is not merely a movement in people's hearts, or a sequence of unconnected events inspired by the Holy Spirit. Its existence is – though we may have to say 'after all' – bound up with the continuities of human life, and provision has to be made so that Christian continuity will run in the right direction. Yet it would never be true to say that Christian institutions developed out of a purely social and historical necessity. Had they done so they would have been much less coherent in themselves because they would have been less obviously coherent with Christ himself. The institution upon which all other Christian institutions are built is the name of Christ, and others are recognised (rather than invented) because they hold Christians to the fact of their standing in Christ. Indeed, as we see especially in baptism and the eucharist, they insist that it is only in union with the crucified Christ that Christians have any standing before God at all. This is a paradoxical way of establishing continuity and order. It certainly anticipates no loss of freedom. The church, according to this way of proceeding, is free to work out for itself how it will conduct itself through time and change, provided only that it remains grounded in the source of its freedom. The problem, as the church proceeds through time and change, is whether that proviso will always be met.

We return then to the idea of a double witness in the New Testament. On the one hand the church is given a remarkable freedom to rethink and reapply the whole complex of sacral ideas in a non-institutional way. On the other we see it becoming aware of the social and historical need for institutions of its own, and making provision for such institutions. We cannot say that these tendencies are consistent with one another, or that the potential clash of motifs is sorted out or reconciled within the New Testament. Perhaps, within the New Testament it is hardly recognised. But both motifs belong to the task which the New Testament generation handed on to the church of later times.

CHAPTER THREE

Towards Definition – A Christian Sacral Priesthood

It is because it became embedded deep down in the life of the Christian peoples, colouring all the *via vitae* of the ordinary man and woman, making its personal turning points, marriage, sickness, death and the rest, running through it year by year with the feasts and fasts and the rhythm of the Sundays, that the eucharistic action became inextricably woven into the public history of the Western world.

Dom Gregory Dix, *The Shape of the Liturgy*

1. The Constantinian Opportunity

Nowhere in the New Testament is it expected that a Christian sacral priesthood would emerge, serving in principle the whole of society. Yet that is what happened and within the space of only three centuries from the resurrection. It is a remarkable fact: it can be deplored, it has undoubtedly brought embarrassment upon the church, and yet it has entered into western culture so deeply that even those who deplore it find it hard to prise themselves loose from it. By a process that was, perhaps, nearer to being inevitable than we care to acknowledge, Christian faith and worship came to take the place in society that older religious practices had taken, and Christian ministers came to be regarded as priests of that society.

The credit and the blame are usually both awarded to the emperor Constantine – that strange mythic figure whose reality seems to elude the most determined attempts to understand him. Was he really capable of the subtle transformation of religion and politics that he is supposed to have brought about? Or was it the media in which he chose to work that provided their own subtlety? We would like to be able to tell the story plainly, without complications, to offer a simple explanation. So we have Constantine the chosen servant of God who, in simple obedience, gave the church its due, recognised its needs and its potential for good and made it free to serve society in the way it was always intended to. We can see him as a sincere Christian who only wanted to do his Christian duty in the role assigned him in society, and who in the main succeeded. Or we can take a negative view, and see him as a crafty statesman who seduced the church and forced it to serve his own political ends. Or again, still negatively, we can believe that he was sincere but mistaken in supposing that his personal syncretistic monotheism was the same thing as Christianity, and we can believe further that failure to correct the mistake at the time was the origin of every compromise that the church has had to blush for since.[1]

At the present time it is the negative versions of the myth that have most appeal. We are more inclined than disinclined to think of the 'Constantinian Settlement' as a fall from grace on the part of the church. It is so far from what the modern church is in reality and yet, through countless social pressures, it makes its uncomfortable claim on us still. We sense that, at a very matter-of-fact and unreflective level, people still want social belonging and Christian belonging to amount to the same thing. They still want to treat Christian ministers as priests to the whole of society. And yet, at a more conscious level, where the consequences of such a unity of church and society are spelt out, people react against it. The vision is refuted by the sociological facts. Church and society are drifting apart in practice, however tenacious the idea remains that they belong together. From a pro-Constantinian point of view the church is in decline. From an anti-Constantinian point of view it is struggling free, with its liberating gospel, from the encumbrances of centuries. Small wonder that the anti-Constantinian view is winning the battle for people's hearts. It takes the same facts that contribute to a sense of failure and charges them with a note of promise. It assures those who find themselves on the margin of society that this is their proper ancestral inheritance. If it was Constantine and his successors who brought the Church into captivity to the demands of politics and culture, these are the days of exodus when the people of God can once again go out into the wilderness to meet him. So it is that current tensions between church and state, current perplexities about baptismal discipline, and current despair at making Christianity and life in society relevant to one another, are all projected upon the church of the Fourth Century to blacken its reputation.[2]

It is undeniable that, once the church does commit itself to a wholehearted participation in the culture of mankind, many problems arise that a disengaged church would not have to face. When the church as an institution starts to work alongside other institutions and in alliance with them it may become a partner in decisions that cannot be made with a completely satisfied conscience. A sense of compromise or frustration may infest its feelings about itself. Worse still, a proper frustration might give way to complacency that, if the church is involved, things must really be all right. Perhaps the church cannot commit itself to society with a whole heart. It has to remain detached. In spite of these things, though, it must not be assumed that the church has been wrong to undertake the task of ministering to a whole society and becoming, in some degree, united with it. Dangerous courses are not necessarily wrong, and not everything that feels uncomfortable is bad. It is equally possible to say that the 'settlement' of which Constantine is the mythic symbol was an opportunity for the church, rather than an imposition upon it, and one which it had a duty under God to respond to.

Liturgical scholars have long recognised that underneath the great developments that took place in Christian worship in the fourth century there were crucial theological convictions. Gregory Dix found the summary phrase for it when he spoke of 'the sanctification of time'.[3] It is true that the theory with which Dix filled out this idea has been severely criticised in recent years. As he expounded it, early Christian worship was eschatological, linking an exiled and world-renouncing church with its heavenly home. There was no place in it for liturgical forms which took the life of mankind in time seriously as matter for holiness. When changes came, as they did in the fourth century, they required a massive change of sensibility, a move from world-renunciation to world-acceptance, 'the translation of worship from the idiom of eschatology to that of time'.

Liturgical historians have come to object to this, on the ground that a temporal liturgy does ante-date the fourth century, and may even go back to Christian continuities with the synagogue, while Alexander Schmemann has shown that the link, which Dix assumed, between eschatology and world-renunciation is neither necessary nor true to the liturgy itself. He recognises a duality in the liturgy, very much in Dix's terms, but not a dualism of opposed alternatives. Rather, for him, the eucharist is included within the rhythm of the liturgy of time as its eschatological fulfilment, and as finding in the liturgy of time its own temporal fulfilment. In this way, although he stands back from Dix, he affirms the centrality of the eucharist to the Christian experience of time, as Dix did, and also one of Dix's key concepts, 'the realisation of heavenly ideals upon earth'.[4]

'It is not surprising', wrote Dix, 'that when the full liberty of public worship in this world was accorded her for the first time under Constantine, the church should have thought it right to realise heavenly ideals so far as might be upon earth.' And not only worship, we might add. The realisation of heavenly ideals upon earth is a perfectly responsible goal for the church to set itself, not only in liturgy, and in its own inner life, but in everything that touches humanity, because God has redeemed humanity and destined it for himself. If this vision hardly appears in the New Testament in any but an apocalyptic form (as when the author of Revelation looks forward to a new heaven and a new earth) there are clear reasons why, in the New Testament period, it could hardly be conceived in any other terms. But as time passed, as circumstances changed, and as the church had to set itself to live for an indefinitely prolonged period in the world, the question of a shared social life on earth that would reflect the Lordship of Christ could not be avoided.

There is a popular vision of Constantine's settlement which has no claim to be taken seriously. It may have been a church battered by persecution, but it was not a naively unworldly, socially marginal church to which Constantine announced his conversion.[5] The new relationship with society which Constantine's accession to power made possible for the church had been preparing for half a century, ever since the emperor Gallienus had given Christians the right to assemble, even if they lacked as yet the right to exist. By the time the persecution of Galerius and Diocletian had broken out, in the early fourth century, Christians made up an estimated ten per cent of the population of the empire. Their presence was to be found, however uneasily, in the army, the magistrature, the imperial civil service and the court. Their basilicas could be seen in prominent public places, even near to Diocletian's own palace. Christian teachers inspired by the catechetical school at Alexandria, had laid claim to the cultural and philosophical riches of hellenism, with as much confidence and as much perception as pagans. The church's life was in no sense hidden from the eyes of man. Toleration gave

Christians the courage, if faith had not already secured it, to develop patterns of communication, among themselves and with society, which immersed them fully in the problems, hopes, and aspirations of humankind. A Christian culture with distinctive Christian social institutions was beginning to grow up, though as yet it lacked legal protection. There were even Christians whose judgement of the situation – and at this distance of time one can hardly say what inhibitions they had to overcome – allowed them to share in pagan society to the extent that they could be educated alongside pagans, entertain and be entertained by them, and even marry into their families. Yet always there would be moments when religious observance would drive the two groups apart, in spite of the fact that both knew that Christian faith and pagan convention were simply not comparable with one another. With pagan practice becoming, in some contexts, socially offensive, and Christian sentiments gaining more and more tolerance or even respect, a process was under way which could hardly end short of a transformed culture in which Christian conduct and liberal sentiment would coincide. Constantine's role in that drama was neither to initiate nor to conclude the process. He removed certain obstacles to its fulfilment, and gave new confidence to those who hoped for it, but at the level of cultural change he really altered nothing. The movement began before him, and developed gradually after him. The penetration of the culture of late antiquity by Christianity was never reducible to imperial policy, however much that might facilitate it from time to time. The essential mechanisms were released by a widespread change of feeling, a new outlook upon life and death to which Christian ideas and practice were congenial. Constantine's actions may have been symptomatic of that change. They certainly did not bring it about.

Again, it was no disabled network of scattered and secretive sects which made up the Catholic Church to which Constantine gave his recognition. It was a church that had struggled hugely over two centuries against persecution from without and heresy and mindless enthusiasm within. It had been forced to develop an internal organisation that was adequate for the task, an international corporate discipline which reflected its common faith in spite of its diverse membership. If we ask how it was that Christianity developed stronger institutions than any other ancient religion, except possibly the emperor cult which was at times indistinguishable from the state, the answer seems to lie in the distinctiveness of the gospel with which the church had been entrusted. This gospel was no local cult, at the service of local needs. It was not a myth to be subsumed under other myths. The church had been charged to bear witness truthfully to the one Lord Jesus Christ, and it was that charge that led both to the development of doctrine and discipline and to the freedom of heart with which Christians faced martyrdom.

So it was that when Constantine came to meet the bishops of the church, and when he tried to put their potential to his own use, he had to recognise that there were limits to their pliability. Not many emerge as unambiguous heroes. There were those who tried to exploit Constantine as much as he exploited them. There were those who were overawed, and those whose discretion gained the upper-hand too soon. Nevertheless, the church had within itself resources to withstand the total takeover that a Constantine or Constantius might think appropriate. There were stubbornly argumentative theologians like Athanasius and Hilary, independent-minded and conservative institutions like the Church of Rome, critical movements like that among the monks in both east and west, and all of these served to show that the church had a life of its own, founded upon the faith entrusted to it, and that its pastoral system was not simply at the service of anyone strong enough to commandeer it.

Undoubtedly the middle of the fourth century was a contentious, uneasy period for the church, and one in which its integrity was tried to the uttermost. Nevertheless we can detect at that time no substantial reaction against the social task which the church had undertaken. Even the monks who stood right outside conventional life, and who shunned ecclesiastical office, were ready to come to the aid of the more compromised churches when they saw their faith threatened. The faith itself did not allow the church to abstract itself from society. The church had maintained against the gnostics for more than two centuries that the whole world was God's creation, that he had redeemed it, and that it was good. Christ was recognised as Lord, not merely of spirits and of human hearts, but of every thing than happened upon earth. Martyrdom had made it plain that the spiritual conflict in which Christians were engaged was bound to be brought out in public. A pagan might invoke the help of God secretly, in order to appear in public with equanimity.[6] A Christian knew himself as one who had submitted to a public truth. One way or another every Christian was called to realise heavenly ideals upon earth.

Besides, as we have already hinted, there was a change in public morale at this time to which the church was bound to minister. The third and fourth centuries AD were a period in which old patterns of confidence had begun to give way, and people had either to exert themselves to defend what had been taken for granted or to go in search of something new. Christian monasticism, in its origins, was a symptomatic response to this situation. It was not, since it could not be at the time, the political establishment of Christianity which led to the monastic reaction of Anthony of Egypt and his followers. Anthony's rejection of conventional society predated the Council of Nicaea by some forty years. It was rather that the bonds that tied individuals to common culture were being loosed, and norms were breaking down, and existential support no longer lay to hand. A conventional way of life no longer kept people free from anxiety. If they wanted power, security, a sense of the favour of God, they had to look for it in those who undertook drastic actions. That did not mean, exclusively, Christian martyrs, confessors, monks and bishops, but it certainly included them. Their neighbours looked upon them with a kind of despairing admiration. There was an authority in them beyond anything hallowed by antiquity. It was not surprising that those whose conduct had shown up the cultural incoherence around them should be expected, when their authority had reached a certain peak, to remake society around their own convictions. And why should any Christian doubt the possibility of doing this! The church's own common discipline had already shown that human life could be brought into a saving subjection to the law of Christ. It's organised almsgiving, its care of the weak, were already widely recognised as tokens of genuine religion. There was no reason why this corporate enterprise should suddenly turn in upon itself when the apparatus of the empire was opened up to it.

Our own position in the late twentieth century is so far distant from those people that, even though we recognise them as our forebears in the faith, we are abundantly free to criticise them. We can see in their case (even if the same thing is hidden in our own) how a tendency to find divine reasons for earthly success allowed them to justify developments that we would be inclined to suspect. We have hindsight, which is always more secure than promise. We look at Constantine from a position of profound disillusionment with politics and politicians. We see in him the beginnings of erastianism – a policy whose failure is apparent all around us. We tell ourselves that things started to go wrong with Constantine.

But none of this justifies us in supposing that the Christian enterprise of the fourth century was not, at least in one respect, grounded in the faith we share across the centuries. Christians then were not free to hold back when the world called them to come forward. They could not be true to the gospel and say at the same time that the predicament of society and culture was not their concern – that they had actually been warned off it. In the service of Christ there are no reserved matters that he keeps back from his church. There are no 'no-go areas' in his kingdom. The priesthood of the church is not concerned merely with certain specifically 'Christian' matters which it has to consecrate to God. It has to make its offering 'in all and for all', holding up to God the whole life of humankind because he is the creator and redeemer of all things.

2. The Eucharistic Priesthood

Questions of principle have to be related to questions of fact. The question of principle here is whether the church can fittingly become an institution of society, but in fact the church of the fourth century was not, and could not become, just any sort of institution. It had a certain distinctive character. It emerged into the Constantinian era at a certain stage in its own development, and the way it found itself at that moment was to determine the kind of response it would be able to make to the demands it now encountered.

How then did it find itself? How did Christians perceive their own Christian belonging? The answer to these questions, however we frame it, has to include a bold reference to the eucharist as the very heart of church life at that time. Whatever individual Christians might do, laity, presbyters or bishops, the church as a whole knew that the eucharistic liturgy was its most characteristic activity. It was for this that God had called it into being; it was upon this that its existence depended. It was at the eucharistic table that Christians rediscovered their common belonging to one another and to Christ. It was here that the stuff of daily life was taken up into the worship of God, and here that human brokenness was repaired by his grace and love. Christian life had then, as it has now, many dimensions – mission, service, education, charity, fellowship, prophecy, pastoral care – but the origin of them all, the point from which each was measured, was the eucharist where all were present in their fullness.

So when society began to open itself in new ways to the church, what the church had to offer was essentially the eucharist, and this was in fact the one element in its life that it was able to hold out to society without embarrassment. Doctrine could be taught only in an atmosphere of controversy, standards of morality might need to be reappropriated under new conditions, and the legal and political competence of the Church was to be disputed for centuries, but there is no trace of uncertainty in the way the church developed liturgically at this time. Christian worship came out into the public world and flourished. As they gathered at the altar of Christ, whatever might be true elsewhere, Christians knew themselves for what they were. This was what they had to offer mankind – the sacrament of Christ himself.

The church then opened up the liturgy to the world, yet even on that point there was not a total alteration from former ways. The manner of eucharistic worship became public in scale rather than private, but the discipline of the eucharistic assembly was not suddenly changed. In one sense, the world as such was still shut out from the mysteries of faith. There was still no way to the eucharist but through baptism, and no way to baptism but through a long and careful catechumenate. The standard of Christian commitment in the fourth century remained very high, and for a long time men and women would have to weigh the options very seriously, whether to become a Christian or not. There is a continuity with the past, here, even the recent past when the church had been bitterly persecuted, which we must not overlook when we ask how the church reacted to its new social opportunity. Bishops availed themselves of their new freedoms in a variety of ways, they allowed themselves to be conscripted for new tasks in society, but they were at pains to ensure that it still made a difference to be a Christian. And all aspects of that difference were concentrated at one point – did you assemble with the others for the eucharist or not?

We return then to the question, what kind of institution could the church become in its new state of enfranchisement? Again, we notice, Christian individuals could become many things – teachers, soldiers, politicians, bureaucrats – but the church was not itself a school, an army, a political party or a civil bureaucracy. Essentially it was a cultic assembly, a people called together for the one task of worshipping God. That was why its role in the emerging culture had to be a religious one, and the institutional form it had to take was that of a priesthood.

Not just any priesthood though – the eucharist had to provide the theological foundation for ideas about the church's priesthood. So far as the church had any theory of its own priesthood it was one that stressed the sacrificial character of the eucharist and the priestly character within the church of the local bishop, at whose hands and through whose prayer the eucharistic offering was made.

Let us leave on one side for a moment the question whether such a theory is valid for the church, whether it is scriptural, whether it is theologically sound. Let us rather take note first of its unsettling, vertiginous character, if it is to be made part of a social theory of the church's life. For to take a priesthood understood in that way and to make it the sacral priesthood of all society is like a king taking a busking comedian and making him, not merely the jester, but the chief of protocol in his court. In a court of that kind, managed by such a person, etiquette and decorum will suddenly seem to be stretched very thin, dependent as they now are on irony as much as good will. A social culture that elects to make the eucharist its cultic centre is one that must become less and less secure in itself the nearer it gets to that centre, because a eucharistic culture is one that mocks our desire to create our own security. It does so by bringing us up against the cross, and it reminds those who want to relax in peace that they stand under the promise of imminent judgement. As often as we eat this bread and drink this cup, we show forth the Lord's death until he come! We are not allowed to settle down. We are held between the astonishing acts of God in past and future.

Now certainly the disturbing elements in eucharistic worship are not the only ones to be found within it. What in one presentation is all sacrifice, penitence and liberation can, in another, be made reassuring, even prudential. Christ enters the world to question it, but also to affirm it. Incarnational theology (and this was the golden age of such theology) tends to stress this affirmatory aspect. It brings forward the Christmas festival to balance Easter, the feast of God's presence with humanity to balance the feast of death and resurrection. Nevertheless the balance has to remain a balance or the eucharist is lost (as in state-maintained Christianity it often actually is). Even within the most complacent presentation of the eucharist the discomfort of Christ's redemptive works remains, challenging our illusion of peace but healing our distress. Underneath the new robes, the ragged motley of the busker remains visible.

The idea of a Christian eucharistic priesthood, then, is socially exciting, but is it theologically legitimate? We must consider this question now, and we can recognise two ways of going about it. Whichever we take we shall be handling ideas and images that have their origin in the New Testament, but in the one we shall try to make New Testament usage definitive for all situations, while in the other we shall allow that the use of imagery has to evolve if the historical character of the church is to be taken seriously. In the second case we still have to distinguish genuine evolution from perversion, critically aware evolution from drift, but the development of doctrine has to be allowed for and examined. It cannot simply be ruled out at the start.

So, when we come to compare developed ideas about eucharist and priesthood in the church with those of the New Testament we must be prepared for some systematic adjustments in the way ideas are employed. Indeed, to speak more boldly, and as we have already argued, the New Testament itself taken as a whole requires such an adjustment. The New Testament is prolific in its use of priestly imagery but, as we have seen, these images are used in ways which are sporadic, uncoordinated and unsystematic. They represent a lively impulse to try out new ideas; an impulse that, if sustained, is bound to lead on to fresh discoveries of meaning. Language is like a fine web of significations stretched over the rather more robust web of human actions and institutions. People try to make the two webs fit one another, to make language serve the needs of practice. They try to give recognition to what practice demands, or exposes to view, by using old words in new combinations. And as the web of action and institution changes, so the web of language changes too. If the post-apostolic church took certain New Testament ideas further than their authors had, that was to be expected and desired, for it is no part of New Testament Christianity to make the New Testament an academic standard of Christian usage – rather the contrary. The dynamism of apostolic Christianity is its greatest social gift to the church of later times, and the unfinished tasks of the New Testament period lay claim upon later Christians to continue and complete them.

New Testament usage in respect of priestly imagery may be

prolific, but it lacks a firm focus within the experience of Christians. It is inchoate, referring to the many moral opportunities of a consecrated life, or it finds its substantiation in a past event – the crucifixion of Jesus – or in heavenly realities – the ascended High Priest, the Lamb slain before the foundation of the world. By contrast eucharistic theology, as it developed, concentrated what had been diffuse; it allowed the heavenly to manifest itself upon earth, and found a single experiential focus for the whole complex of priestly images in the eucharist itself. Hebrews and Revelation had shown that priesthood and sacrifice found their fullness in Christ crucified. Paul and 1 Peter had suggested that priestliness was the very stuff of Christian living, and that what had once been established by Christ's death and resurrection had now to be lived out by Christians. But there was no consistency in the way these perceptions were put to use, no single idea that was definitive for all the rest. If the matter had been left at that stage Christian ideas about priesthood would have been like an attempt to draw a circumference without a centre.

The ideas of the New Testament, its hints, its flashes of wisdom, its excursions of the analogical imagination, are compelling but tantalising as long as they remain in an unsystematic state. The church, however, has never felt itself constrained to leave them like that. It has striven within itself to work them up into coherent doctrine. The quest for coherence has appeared perfectly legitimate in the case of the doctrines of God, of Christ and of the Holy Spirit. Why not, then, of the nature of priesthood in Christ?

Like a jigsaw, of which the pieces fall into place, once the key piece has been identified, the Christian theology of priesthood begins to be consolidated once it is recognised that the eucharist is its centre. In various ways but with an unabashed certainty the church came to see the eucharist as 'the sacrifice' that it had been instituted to offer. Here its common life, its organisation, its moral struggle and its public witness, its summons to mutual love and its programme of mutual support all came together in a single expressive act. For here too, and above all, the church shared in the life and self-offering of Christ. Here the historical self-offering was made actual in the present, and earthly aspirations were taken up into the intercession of the heavenly priest. At this moment the very idea of priesthood is appropriated by the church in a fresh and vigorous way, to illuminate the meaning of its gospel and its task.

However, the theological fecundity of the eucharist, seen in this way, ought not to blind us to a difficulty that accompanies it. We can put it like this: which is the true cult? The universalised cult which the eucharist now signifies symbolically, or the particular cult which it simply *is*? The images of the New Testament encourage us to see the whole action by which we are saved as a cosmic cultus, the offering and acceptance of the sacrifice of Christ. They also speak of Christian moral action as the offering of a sacrifice and suggest that this too is in some way part of Christ's cosmic work. The perceptions here are theological. Language is stretched to follow theology. But in the case of the eucharist there is a level of perception at which language is not stretched at all. To any analyst of social behaviour, and setting aside any theological considerations, the eucharist simply is a cult, a priestly action. That is what it must appear to be to any detached observer. Paul had already taken the risk of bringing this kind of perception into play when he compared the eucharist with pagan sacrifice, the table of the Lord with the table of demons (1 Cor. 10.20). Nevertheless the equivocation involved in this is quite unsettling, once attention is drawn to it. The cult discernible to social analysis and the cult discernible to faith are not the same thing. They have to be distinguished.

And yet they are one – they interpenetrate one another. That, at least, we have to say if sacramental theology is true theology, and if Christ who fills all things has also 'placed himself in the order of signs'.[8] The universal cultus finds its focus in a symbol which is congruent with it. In this way it lays claim to all reality and in particular all social and cultural reality. It demands that the system of human devices which would be there, whatever was true in respect of God and humanity, shall open itself up to this particular claim to universal truth – the truth of Christ. It uses human language to say, 'Behold your God', and human signs to manifest the presence of God.

In the eucharist, therefore, a sociological understanding and a theological understanding of what is happening are linked together and made to inform one another. The eucharist is a priestly act in the neutral sense that it articulates something that people regard as sacred. It is also priestly in the theologically affirmative sense that it displays the priesthood of Christ and his church sacramentally. And while there is danger in this equivocation, there is also power in it.

In the fourth century it was this powerful equivocation which allowed the Christian theology of priesthood to become socially effective. If the eucharist provided the experiential centre for the church's theological understanding of priesthood, it also provided the sociological base for its exercise of priesthood. It allowed theology to take hold of society institutionally.

We have seen that in the New Testament period some initial recognition was given to the church as an institutional structure, with ministerial office exercised by those called and designated for the purpose. This too develops, alongside theology, in post-apostolic times. The need for *episcope*, pastoral oversight, came to be realised by the concentration of responsibility in one man, the *episcopos* or bishop. The need for eldership, that is for leadership and care by senior members of the body, was realised in the presbyterate. *Diakonia*, service, care for the social and bodily needs of Christians, was provided through the office of the deacon. The development of these offices reflects a developing social awareness in the Church. And just as Christians experienced the nature and power of their Christian calling when they shared in the eucharist, so these offices were given clearer definition in relation to Christ by the specific way in which they were exercised within the eucharist itself. Liturgical functions are never merely liturgical, as though the liturgy were an end in itself. What the liturgy presents, and establishes as true, has to be carried through into every kind of human situation. So the pastoral and social relationships of the church are also manifested in the liturgy and the relationships which the liturgy symbolises have to be made effective in practice. That is why the bishop, the president of the church, is also the president at the eucharist. Because the presbyters share with him in oversight they stand with him and join with him when he offers thanks to God. Because the deacons are the servants or 'waiters' of the church they collect the gifts of the congregation, and distribute the sacrament to its members. As for the laity, far from being passive recipients or spectators at an official function which the clergy carry out, unilaterally dependent upon them, they are the foundation of the whole building. The liturgy has the form and meaning that we find in it because of what they bring into it and carry from it.

The whole church through its various orders participates in the eucharistic offering, and in that sense no Christian is outside the Church's priesthood, but participates 'each in his office',[9] or according to his or her assigned liturgy. Lay people (the offerers, the *prospherontes*)[10] offer by bringing and giving up to God their gifts of bread and wine. The deacon offers by presenting these gifts to the bishop at the holy table. The bishop offers, and the presbyters with him, through the eucharistic prayer in which the gifts are made over to God with thanksgiving, to become the sacrament of Christ's body and blood. All share, no one is excluded, although there are differences of calling within the one body. The universal priesthood of the Church, which is certainly not fully contained within the eucharist, is nevertheless displayed fully by means of it.

Why then – and by the fourth century this was already current – is the bishop or presiding presbyter at the eucharist especially called the priest? Is it possible to hold that the eucharist exhibits the fullness of the universal priesthood to which the Church witnesses, when within it and seemingly cutting across this universality, one person or only a few are specially designated priests?

The point is vital if we are to understand how the Church's ministry to society developed. As society and Church grew closer together it was this specially designated group – the bishops and presbyters – who were to become the sacral priests of each community. It was their task to articulate the relationship between God and society. It was to be through their ministry, initiating, responding, symbolising and focussing, that the gospel was to gain a purchase on the total life of humankind. But they were able to do this because the same social function had already been anticipated within the Church in the days when it stood apart from society – when it was, so to speak, a society in itself. Even when Christian culture and fellowship were distinguished by their separateness, the leader of eucharistic worship had already come to be called a priest.[11] If one does not wish to denounce this development it is tempting at this point to turn aside in pursuit of a theological justification for it. Can it be shown that the specific priesthood of the called and ordained minister is not theologically inconsistent with the universal priesthood of the Church, that it is integral with it, or even that it is in some way essential to it? In the end it may be necessary to attempt such an argument. Nevertheless, at this stage, we ought to resist the temptation. We are not dealing here with some obvious continuity of language, but with equivocation, just as we are when we speak of sacrifice in the eucharist, applying the same term both to the sign and the thing signified. The eucharistic minister is called a priest in the first instance simply by virtue of the position he or she occupies within the structure of the community. The word is used anthropologically before – and for that matter whether or not – it is used theologically. What the minister does and the relationships it establishes are so far analogous to what priests do, that he or she can properly be called a priest as well.

We can put it like this. The necessity of priesthood operates within all societies, and its effect is to produce differentiation of functions within them. Priesthood is primarily an articulation of social relationships in such a way that the sacred becomes manifest through them. This necessity cannot be avoided within a certain society simply because that society is regarded as priestly in its totality. Even though the whole church is priestly in a theological sense, it will still need its own peculiar priests in a sociological sense. This kind of priesthood – priesthood understood as a form of social articulation – will be present wherever church life achieves some degree of social permanence. It will be present whether the word 'priest' is used or not. It will be present whether it is deliberately recognised and provided for, or systematically covered over and denied. It will arise through deliberate and concerted action, or through unconscious manipulation, but it cannot be avoided.

What do we gain by recognising this? First, we gain self-awareness. We shall not entertain illusions of freedom from priestly structure when in fact we have it in substance and only the accidental features of it are different from those of others. We shall be free to face the necessity, and ask ourselves how God is to be served through it. And we should be able to see that this requires a dialogue of theological and sociological perceptions. Theology cannot neutralise sociological reality, but it ought not to be controlled by it either, as is likely to happen when church structure is treated as a non-theological factor. Each has to be recognised for what it is.

From this point of view the perceived equivocation about priestly imagery in Christian use is a sign of health. We are having to make an uncomfortable distinction, and sustain it against the passion for simplicity that religious people are so easily swayed by. But at least by now the feel of this equivocation should have become familiar. Is it not simply another form of the recurrent, jarring doublet – that the church has to be both and simultaneously a divinely constituted organism and a human institution, that the gospel of Christ has to be spoken in human words, even though human words must inevitably distort it, that human beings have to respond to God though every response falls short of God and so partakes of the character of idolatry? As we face the question of the church's priestly calling in society, all these issues come back with a new urgency.

But perhaps, at the same time, we can claim that if there is any answer to this problem we ought to be getting nearer to finding it. Discussions of principle seem to lead every time to contradictions and equivocations. We end up repeatedly arguing that two things which seem to be incompatible with one another have to be held together. But if this demand to hold the incompatible together arises not simply from the gospel, but from the fact that the gospel calls the church into existence, then the answer may lie not in some abstract theory, but in the concrete reality of the church. Theology may insist that we must have a church that does not contradict the gospel, but what if the gospel is itself subversive?

CHAPTER FOUR

Priesthood and the Subversive Gospel

the Cross an example
of the power of art to transcend timber
R. S. Thomas, *Good Friday*

1. Contradiction

Christians make a good deal of the image of the newborn child. They find a peculiar pathos in the image of Christ as a baby, and they like to see themselves as newborn children in a spiritual sense as well. The child's condition corresponds so very closely with that of a believer – total vulnerability, but contained by, measured against, total parental care. A baby does nothing for itself, it is innocent of all designs, and yet by merely existing it makes a massive claim to consideration and respect. The Christian doctrine of grace represents Christians in very much these terms.[1] But, in real life, childhood is a temporary condition. As the child develops it finds that some degree of autonomy is forced upon it, and that, correspondingly, its parents are not there only for its own sake. Their indulgence and protection begin to be qualified in various ways. The child has to learn to take care of itself, to guard itself from the world, but also guard itself from the parents who are no longer to be looked to for everything. It begins to develop habits of response, ploys, stratagems, techniques of avoidance and evasion. It learns how to present itself and hide itself at the same time and in the same action. Its skin thickens. It develops a shell.

That seems to be the story of the church as well. Initially it behaved with innocent bravado, with uncalculating enthusiasm. All it had to do was trust God and live out the meaning of that trust. But then the church too discovered that it had to live with its own autonomy, it had to be responsible for itself, it had to guard itself from errors within and misunderstanding without. To use a phrase that only a worldly church could use, it had to 'come to terms with' its worldly existence. Church and child alike witness to a universal human tendency to develop a carapace around original innocence. Something that began in a very uncomplicated way – sheer delight and acceptance of life – gives way to suspicion, caution and the demand for proof.

> Issues from the hand of time the simple soul
> Irresolute and selfish, misshapen, lame,
> Unable to fare forward or retreat,
> Fearing the warm reality, the offered good,
> Denying the importunity of the blood.
>
> (T. S. Eliot, *Animula*)

Worldly wisdom does not abolish the image of the child, but suffers it to lodge with us as something compromised, out of place. When we are reminded of that sometime innocence we feel more keenly our present fallenness. It cannot be reversed and there is no one on earth who has not been affected by it. Even religion, even the church, has been affected by it. And yet, surely, someone will say ('surely' – that infallible signal of a question being begged) the church at least is not meant to be like that. The church is a sign of redemption, not just another witness to the fall. The way of all flesh may run towards organised self-protection, but the church represents the liberty of the Spirit and it loses itself when it ceases to be free. The idea that the church is an organisation too and that its existence has an institutional shape remains deeply disturbing to many Christians. The ministry of the church, with its traditional structure, its prerogatives and duties, is something to be questioned, a cause of embarrassment. For it seems that this historic ministry has developed along with the hardening of the church. It is itself part of the church's shell. How then can we claim that it is God's priesthood? We must put this question as sharply as we can, not so that we can take one side against another but so that we can admit before we go any further that there *are* two sides, and that they are not to be lightly reconciled. Christianity is deeply contradictory. It has its place, its only possible place, in the fallen world, and yet it is called to testify to God's victory over that world. Its great moments, the moments from which it is meant to live, are those when the heavens open, God dwells among his people, and all the promises of history are fulfilled. And yet the church's day-to-day existence is simply that, day to day. Heaven remains resolutely closed, and the course of history continues. If God is still really present in the church it is in a wonderfully paradoxical and hidden way.

We are not going to escape from this paradox by settling for one position against the other. Simplicities of that kind are not attainable. Heaven is not evidently open, yet we cannot settle for a closed-off and totally autonomous earth. Innocence is not to be recovered, but we cannot betray innocence and remain the Church of God. That leaves only one possibility – if it is a possibility: to live with the contradiction, commit ourselves to both positions and hold the two together. We have to live as witnesses to the redemption of Christ, even under the conditions of the fall. We have to sustain the vision of innocence, even in the midst of experience, exposing it to view by means of the very knowledge that experience itself has given us.

Can that be done? It may be that social analysis can show us a way.

2. Anti-Structure

Like many of my own generation I was called up to do National Service in the Army. My basic training happened near Richmond in Yorkshire, in a district of great natural beauty. What better place, one might ask, for the open-air life of a young soldier? But more exactly it was at Catterick Camp, and the name of Catterick rings a rather different bell. The camp was then (whatever it may be now) a superb example of advanced architectural blight. Lines of mean barrack-room huts dating back to 1914 promised the worst, and after we had been there a day or two we knew that the promise was going to be kept to the letter.

We reported, we were assembled, and our lives were taken over. In the space of twenty-four hours we were reduced to a state of extreme shock and confusion. We were sheared of our hair like sheep, stripped of our civilian clothes, and dressed in shapeless denims; we were lined up and made to move about to the noise of threats and curses; we were forced to work harder and longer than ever before, and we simply lost our bearings. Our sense of time broke down, nothing was predictable any more, we had no leisure, and when we were left without supervision we had to work desperately to be ready for the moment when it would return. Our sense of standards also broke down. There were no values to which we could appeal, no guarantees of any kind. We grieved with a deep and painful grief.

How could we relieve our desperation? Looking back on it now I see that two kinds of relief were open to us. No doubt those who devised this initiation intended at least one of them. If not, they were quite as sadistic as they appeared to be at the time. They wanted us to become proper soldiers. If we could learn to dress and drill and respond to orders like soldiers, then we might begin to discover where we were. That, as it now seems, must have been the object of this assault upon us, to deprive us of our civilian mentality, to show us that we were no longer the collection of apprentices and workmen, gentlemen and scholars that we imagined we were, to reduce us all to a common adaptability, and then to make soldiers of us. Civilians are of no use in the army. Before we could really belong in the army we should have to lose ourselves and find ourselves afresh. We should have to become nothing, in order to become something new.

But the other way of relief lay much closer at hand and as far as I could see it had nothing to do with the intentions of our persecutors. We would discover for ourselves that peculiarly subversive outlook that private soldiers have among themselves. That is to say we could discover one another, not as civilians or as soldiers, but simply as men, and in doing that we might recover what 'they' seemed determined to take away from us, our sense of humanity. It was nobody's job to explain this to us. Nobody had planned it. It emerged incidentally, and we had to discover it for ourselves, discover it in purely practical ways without reflecting on what we might be achieving. But fairly rapidly we just got to know one another as human beings. The basic demand was that people should do their share of the work, pitch in and not 'skive', and not get the rest of us into trouble; and (here was where we had to become resourceful) there was no assured system for achieving that. No one could pull rank on anyone else. We could only insist that people should take us as they found us, with kindness if they could, with cheerfulness if there was room for cheerfulness, and by a kind of bullying consensus if all else failed. Remarkably and quite rapidly this is what began to happen. We achieved an unheralded, unpredictable but real corporate spirit. Things like this, of course, can be idealised. We speak of *camaraderie*, we conjure up warm memories, and we forget that human personalities left to themselves without a framework of convention are rather like rocks in an avalanche colliding with one another even while they maintain unity of direction. What emerges on these occasions can sound comfortably commonplace, if one forgets the strain out of which it comes. People are people, especially when they're in trouble; they need one another and can help one another, and sometimes all the more because conventions do not stand in the way. So it was here, in spite of the pain. As long as we were neither soldiers nor civilians, there would be no barriers between us, certainly no social barriers. If that left us feeling undefended, sometimes it also made us available to one another, and we could take care of our common needs by all kinds of spontaneous devices.

Most of us have been initiated into something, at one time or another – at least into such common conditions as marriage and parenthood or the curiously closed societies of school, office and factory. Most of us then have experienced the shift from one set of conventions to another that accompanies this process, and the giddy moment between them when we are given up to fresh discoveries and the pain of free expression. Later on we forget the experience because it has made us what we now are. If I now recall my initiation into our conscript army with a certain vividness it is probably first of all because, like a bad inoculation, it didn't take – because the attempt to restructure our existence worked only at a superficial level, leaving the long-term process of self-discovery unaffected. The experience stands out now as an immense effort, unworthy of nearly everyone who took part in it, and certain to fail. But it does stand out, a vivid memory because so isolated from other memories. Because I recall it as something inflicted, and not absorbed into the system, it remains like a mass of experimental data, awaiting analysis.

That must be why it all came back to me so concretely when I first read Victor Turner's book *The Ritual Process*[2] and recognised that the very things he was writing about – mainly initiation rites in tribal Africa – had been practised on me not sixty miles from where I had been brought up. I too had been put through these exotic rituals. I too, with thousands like me, had been made to see that the world we construct for ourselves is not the only possible one, and that there is sometimes more than one place to stand when making the choice between them.

No doubt Turner was saying something well known to anthropologists, and I have come across it in schematic summaries many times since. But originally, taken with the experience I had once had and now found remarkably illuminated, it came not as a formula but more as a questioning of formulae. The conventional wisdom about institutions had been exploded.[3] We tend to think that institutions give shape to human relationships always in the same way; that there may be many institutional patterns, but they are always held together by the same structural principles. Turner simply questioned that.

Schematic presentation is unavoidable in an essay like this, so, even if with misgiving, we must attempt it. An initiation process, like basic training in the army or puberty rituals in tribal societies, takes someone from one position in the structure of society and then places them in another and different position within the same structure.[4] In tribal rituals, boys become men. In Catterick camp civilians become soldiers. But between these initial and final states there is a period when the initiate is in a quite distinct condition – quite separate from what we call normal life with its normal expectations and guarantees. This is called the *liminal* condition[5] because it lies on the doorstep of organised, systematic society. It was this condition that we conscripts and recruits had experienced when we were neither civilians nor soldiers, lacking all assurance as to where we stood and forced to find our salvation in sheer humanity. And the liminal condition is always, one way or another, what we had found it to be – a liberation from structure and an exposure to brute humanity, personal, spontaneous, and raw.

Of course, people all experience and value freedom and spontaneity, but for the most part they fail to notice how far they qualify their approval of these things, how careful they are to keep freedom within boundaries. Ritual processes like my Catterick initiation force us into awareness of the polar opposition between the two – the opposition of structure and anti-structure.[6] On the one hand lies organised human existence, the world of enduring and socially supported relationships, of firm expectations, assigned roles, guaranteed status and hierarchical chains of command. On the other lies the condition Turner calls *communitas*,[7] the anti-structural condition, in which firm expectations are no longer firm and can be questioned, and mutually adjusted roles no longer fit. Human personality, when the conditions suit, can shrug off the system of rules it has respected and perhaps taken for granted, and emerge in a new way, immediate, potentially threatening but also potentially very generous. Personality is never simple in itself, but in structured society we can sometimes harmonise our own complexities with the complexities of routine and convention and so, on these occasions, get what we want at the least cost in energy. In anti-structural situations this harmony breaks down, and complex personalities have to come to terms with one another through direct encounter. The framework is now simpler, but the task is much more complicated – potentially enriching, but potentially exhausting.

In the ritual process as Turner describes it people pass from structure into a phase of naked anti-structure and then back into structure again, at a point in advance of the one they left. The process is not cyclic but progressive. The anti-structural, liminal phase allows those who pass through it to change, and it allows the society from which they have been parted to receive them back as changed. They no longer occupy the same position in society's structure, and their experience of that structure from now on will be different. We can, and commonly do, focus on that change of social role or status. The spinster is now a wife, the junior member has now been promoted, the common citizen is now an elected representative. But we may fail to notice that between these two substantive positions there is an interval in which the person is neither, in which he or she is 'nothing', and it is because for a time he or she is recognised as 'nothing' that a subsequent return as something new is tolerable. That much is necessary for society, if it is to adjust its response to people in new roles, but in truth the one who undergoes this change needs it even more. He or she has to find some way of letting the old go and the new arrive establish itself. The liminal phase (even if it is as brief as a stag party) provides a moment when he or she can be defined as nothing, neither one thing nor another, because at least for a moment nothing is settled, possibilities are still open in several directions, and the question can be faced afresh, who am I? and what am I for?

One can hardly speak of these things without invoking Christian concepts. How can those who have allowed themselves to recognise their own nothingness allow themselves to be set again among the substances of the world unless they have trust in the one 'who calls into being the things that are not as though they were' (Rom. 4.17)? And what kind of liminality was it that Jesus called his disciples into when they forsook everything to follow him (Luke 5.11 & 28)? And what sort of redefinition of oneself is it that Paul points to when he says, 'If anyone is in Christ there is a new creation' (2 Cor. 5.17)?

Perhaps we can allow ourselves one probing guess, at this stage, into the exegesis of these texts. They represent the effect of faith upon human lives, but not, as we might suppose, in moral terms – for then they would have to be universally and perpetually applicable – but in *social* terms. They say something (among other things) about the social meaning of discipleship. But before we run ahead any further into the application of these ideas to the church we ought to pursue the ideas themselves a little further, if only to avoid certain mistakes about where they may lead.

First we need to distinguish between *liminality* and *marginality*.[8] Liminality, as we have seen, is a condition in which social structures cease to operate in the normal way. It is anti-structural – a condition in which it is safe and perhaps necessary to survival to question socially accepted patterns. In the liminal condition you can challenge, with as much daring as you can muster, the emperor's claim to be wearing clothes, provided, that is, you are ready to admit that you have no clothes yourself. Marginality, in at least one way, is quite different. It corresponds simply to a structural perception that certain people or activities are not very significant for the interests that control the structure. They are part of the scheme. They know as we all know where they belong, but it doesn't make much difference whether they are there or not. Economically, or politically, they don't count. They are the small change of the structured world.

Marginality then approximates to nothingness in the sense that it can be ignored by those who have substance. The nothingness of the liminal condition, however, is a challenge to everyone and everything to justify its claim to be something. It is a reminder to us all of the nothingness out of which we have been brought.

Once the distinction is made it is clear that the two conditions are not synonymous and need not coincide. Initiation rituals, and the liminal condition which is essential to them, are not at all marginal to the societies which observe them. They are major social institutions. And it follows from this that if the church is committed by its own theological calling to a certain anti-structural or liminal condition, it is by no means committed *ipso facto* to social marginality.[9]

Secondly we need to distinguish between liminality and anti-structure. The approach I have outlined to this way of thinking, through the example of a military passage rite, has meant that we have come upon the two ideas together and at a place where no distinction needed to be made between them. For such liminality is *pure* anti-structure. It arises when structural relationships are simply suspended or abolished. Nevertheless anti-structure is not restricted to liminality. It is not at all that every kind of human association must be either wholly structural, or wholly anti-structural. Flexibility in human affairs can be achieved without every time demanding that all existing definitions shall be lifted and every thing examined afresh. It is rather that structure is followed, shadowed, *haunted* by anti-structure. Wherever structure is found in human relationships a potential, and sometimes actual, anti-structure can be discovered along with it, and this is often essential to the working of the scheme. Human beings devise all kinds of ways for getting things done, very necessary and proper to the world's work. Nevertheless, unless these devices are menaced ever so gently with irony or lightened by conviviality they will fail to serve humanity.

Marriage will serve as an example. Nothing could be more institutional in the way it is set up and recognised within society. The married couple itself is a social institution. Then there is a secondary institutional character in the way husband and wife conceive their mutual roles and carry them out. Yet marriage would not be marriage if these institutional definitions, these structural elements, became an exhaustive description of what was actually expected, as though the whole thing could be worked out automatically according to the rules. Marriage actually offers to provide an institutional context for the love of two people, who take one another 'for better for worse'. It brings them together in order to expose them to one another in all their moods and sufferings in a far more unrestrained way than in many less institutional arrangements. And this anti-structural element is in no way an occasional or even inevitable by-product of the institution. It is what the institution itself proposes.

Liminality then is not to be identified with anti-structure. It is a limiting case of anti-structure – a condition in which at least one aspect of structure is totally suspended. But totality is not always demanded, and this too will be important for any application of this kind of thinking to the church. It is easy, armed with the right texts, to conceive of the church as pure *communitas*, an association without structure of any kind. The fact that such a thing is impossible (at least without some external pressures towards it) does not stop people judging the church by such a standard. But to say that total anti-structure is impossible is not at all to deny the anti-structural demand of Christian faith. Rather, the demand must be seen as pointing to a fruitful *union* of structure and anti-structure if it is in fact taken as a demand laid upon the church.

How then does an anti-structural demand appear in human relationships? Structures normally take the form of settled patterns, hierarchies, chains of command, distinctions of authority and status. By contrast anti-structure works towards equality, it forces people to obtain the consent of others and not assume it, and it gives common action an experimental, unpredictable quality. Structure rests on power, while anti-structure exposes a common powerlessness. Structure seeks to exhibit and reinforce differences – rich from poor, male from female, familiar from stranger – while anti-structure seeks to minimise differences and to strip away the signs and badges that enforce them. Structure means predictability, anti-structure spontaneity. Structure ministers to self-assurance and pride, anti-structure encourages humility and self-discovery. Structure insists on the functionality of human arrangements – are they efficient, economical, proportionate to their aim? Anti-structure accepts and even delights in the dysfunctional.[10] It loves magnificence and mocks at the concept of *waste*. When the woman in the gospels 'wasted' her valuable ointment on Jesus, it was structure which asked what this had achieved, and anti-structure which pointed to its symbolic meaning and to the love it had expressed.

These tendencies find their goal in the liminal condition, wherever that condition appears. To say it again, liminality is not the whole of anti-structure, but it does expose its intent and direction. That, among other values, is its *diagnostic* value. We see what anti-structure is working towards, when we see what liminality actually involves – the suspension of social differences, the abandonment of hierarchy, mutual subjection, mutual obedience, the willing acceptance of pain and disadvantage, the stripping off of marks of distinction even to the point of actual nakedness, isolation from daily life, homelessness, hunger, uncertainty as to past or future. But let us recall that this condition is not sought for itself. It is rather pursued and affirmed as the nothingness out of which new substance is to be created. And more generally, anti-structure is valued because it opens human affairs up to fresh perceptions and new experiences.

3. Christian Anti-Structure

The parallels with the organisation of the early church, with its practical demands upon its members and even with its theology are reasonably obvious here. When Jesus insists that the disciples must deny themselves, and take up their cross (Mark 8.34), he is calling them into this kind of anti-structural position. When he insists that Christian leaders must not rule like the kings of the Gentiles, lording it over their subjects, but must be the servants of all (Mark 10.44), he is planting an anti-structural mine under the foundations of normal social relationships. When the status of Christians in relation to God is contrasted with their despised condition in the world (1 Cor. 1.26–28), or when Paul insists on his nakedness, hunger and suffering as marks of his apostleship (2 Cor. 11.23–30), then the calling of Christians is being set forth as an anti-structural impulse in human experience. The gospel, at root, in respect of those things which make it a gospel of good news, is through and through anti-structural. It calls people to discover status actually in their lack of status, riches in their poverty, security in their loss, health in their suffering, or (to be less brief) through the action of God upon those who are in such conditions. The gospel runs askew to social custom. It 'turns the world upside down' (Acts 17.6). Jesus refuses to be labelled (John 8.25). He cannot be defined by a title whose meaning is already fixed. He will not justify his authority to those who might confirm it or compromise with it by an act of their own authority. He cannot, nor can the Christian, be fitted into any human system.

'The wind blows where it wills, and you hear the sound of it but you do not know where it comes from or where it is going: So is every one who is born of the Spirit' (John 3.8).

If that is the nature of the gospel it has to be the nature of the church as well. The church too, in some respect essential to its existence, must be anti-structural. Practically speaking, that means that it must resist any attempt to define its tasks in purely social-structural terms. It has to resist the suggestion that it is *primarily* an organisation, even when this is done euphemistically through the use of words like 'community' and 'fellowship'. It has to resist all attempts, hostile or friendly, to delimit its role in society, and to show where its competence begins and ends. It has to resist, to the point of contradiction, the notion that ministers of the gospel are essentially functionaries and organisers in the church – leaders, managers or rulers. Every one of these proposals, however innocently meant, and however justified by the facts, is an attempt to take the church into the system where it does not finally belong.

There is, of course, a simple theological reason for resistance. We could call it the only serious theological reason for anything – that God has to be recognised as God. And God cannot be recognised as active in human lives if human life is conceived from the outset in purely structural terms. The God who acts upon humankind only through structure, and who is therefore part of the total structure himself, even if he is seen as its crown and all-inclusive canopy,[11] is indistinguishable from an idol. He cannot be *recognised* as God. So the recognition of God calls out for anti-structure. Just as anti-structure allows people to respond to other people in freedom and spontaneity, so it allows us to recognise God in his freedom, and to respond with an answering freedom. God and God's actions always elude our attempts to fix their occasion and meaning, and for that reason the most convincing pointer to the action of God will always have to appear to us as a challenging question, a summons to let go, or a judgement upon the ineffectiveness of human devices.

And yet by now it should be quite clear that we are not going to escape human devices. There will be no church and no ministry of the gospel unless there is institution, organisation and leadership, with some kind of social definition. Furthermore, the gospel, though it challenges every kind of confidence in the structures of society, is still a charter of commitment to society itself, structure and all. For it is to humankind in its totality, including all its social responsibilities and relationships, that the gospel is addressed.

The gospel has no bias to anti-structure as such (in spite of any conclusions so far drawn). The gospel requires anti-structure only for the sake of God. The liminal condition is not itself a divinely ordered condition. It may give scope to generosity and love, but it also gives scope to viciousness and personal assertiveness. The best and the worst kinds of human behaviour can be pursued in spontaneity. The anti-structural demand of the gospel, then, is not a plea that we shall live in this totally ambiguous condition for its own sake, but a demand, rather, that all human life, as pursued in all social contexts, shall be opened up to God.

That is why it is so important that we should see human life as a whole which continually unites structural and anti-structural experiences. It is not a matter of choosing between them. They are like the two poles of a magnet which have to be kept apart but also have to remain connected with one another. Structure and anti-structure reach out to one another in human affairs, and neither is human without the other.[12] Structure on its own is mechanical. Anti-structure on its own is chaotic. Only together can they provide that order within freedom and freedom within order which is essential to true humanity. The gospel affirms this mutual belonging, more obviously against the pride, complacency and oppressiveness that accompany structure, but equally against the irresponsibility and despair that the total absence of structure can lead to. Of course it does more than attempt to hold the balance. It affirms the fruitful tension between structure and anti-structure in order to consecrate it to God.

The church and its ministry, then, cannot be described adequately either in pure institutional nor in pure anti-institutional terms. Neither aspect is primary, but both are necessary to a whole perception. The church cannot escape awareness of itself; it has to identify itself, organise its proper activities, enter into a constructive relationship with society. It has to be in one sense at home in the world, even while in the same moment, by the same impulse, it is not at home. For its being in the world is not to give comfort to worldly self-satisfaction. Its calling is to point beyond the world, and also (because in this respect too it is wholly one with the world) to point beyond itself.

The church, let us say then, is to be an institution that points beyond itself. That is the character of its institutional *raison d'être*. That at least limits the kind of institution it can be. Things point beyond themselves to the extent that they operate as symbols. Symbols offer something to the human thirst for rational form, but they do not satisfy it. They say, by presenting themselves as symbols, that, in the matter which they symbolise, reason cannot be wholly satisfied. Symbols allow us to identify what we are dealing with, but not to imagine we have mastered it. Rather they invite us to relax our search for mastery and become receptive – receptive to a meaning which they have to offer but do not pretend to define. The church too can be seen as a symbol in this sense, and its institutional form is to be controlled by that fact. It takes an institutional form for the sake of its symbolic function.

These things are apparent in certain aspects of church life, less so in others. Worship exhibits the principle most fully. Liturgy by its very nature points worshippers beyond itself. (In practice, of course, this may not happen. Liturgy can be turned into a substitute for God, or it can be so devised that it turns the worshippers back upon themselves so that they celebrate themselves. The difference between good and bad liturgy usually rests upon these distinctions.) Liturgy seeks to articulate the human approach to God, not so that this approach can be described but so that it can take place. The offer of the Body and Blood of Christ in the eucharist is not an invitation to intellectual debate but to participation, and to understanding only in so far as it serves participation. Words of praise and adoration are not designed to encourage us to ask what we are doing, but to do it in a way which engages the intellect and transcends it at the same time.

The church is also called to teach and to proclaim. It lives by doctrine, and doctrine too has to be understood symbolically. That does not mean that the matters of which doctrine treats are 'not real'. Symbol is a means of signification, not a judgement on the status of what is signified. Doctrine works symbolically in that through it both the positive and negative capabilities of understanding are kept in play. Christian doctrine seeks to articulate an understanding of Christian truth, but it also seeks to indicate that every understanding, even this one, is inadequate to its object. Perhaps the whole of Christian doctrine can be reduced to a single proposition, that it is not we who take hold of God but he who takes hold of us through Jesus Christ. That single statement has to be worked out in moral and ascetical terms – those perhaps first of all – but then also in intellectual terms. We need to perceive its implications for all that our intellect comprehends. We also need to understand the way in which God's truth lies beyond our comprehension. In this sense the institutional forms of doctrine – creed, dogma and scripture – are to be taken as institutions and symbols too that point beyond themselves.

Can we in this way hope to resolve the sense of contradiction which has pursued all our insistence on the institutional character of the church? We have argued that the church must take its place among the institutions of society, not only because of a kind of sociological inevitability but also for the sake of society itself. We have also argued that the call of God in the gospel of Christ is one which transcends human institutions and which sets us free for the venture of love beyond anything so far determined or achieved. And it seems that, frankly, there can be no church at all if these two conditions are not met, however opposed they seem to be.

For in the gospel we have something more than a preference for anti-structure or an insistent counsel that it is wise not to rely on institutions. We have a quite specific anti-structural principle to which testimony has to be borne, consistently and perseveringly. Turner's word is applicable here, 'The ultimate desideratum, however, is to act in terms of communitas values while playing structural roles'.[13] If the gospel has been given merely to produce a momentary explosion in human affairs, then it could be stated in totally non-institutional terms, or even not stated at all – the event would be enough. But because the gospel has to be witnessed to afresh, in every age and really in every human situation, it has to provide for its own continuity in the world. That continuity can be found only in a social institution – an institution which accepts social structure and which has its own structural elements, but which is able, such is the character of these elements, to point continually beyond itself to the liberating presence of God. In principle there is nothing contradictory about this. Freedom, if it is to endure, requires form. Truth, including the truth that lies beyond our grasp, needs an abiding witness if it is to be abidingly recognised.

All the same it follows from this that the church cannot be just any kind of institution. Liberty and form may be necessary both to society as a whole and to the church, but, in a pragmatic perspective, such a necessity always turns out to be paradoxical or plainly impossible. We know how institutions become rigid as people's interests get bound up with them, how they become instruments of self-defence or repositories of social power. Whenever the church's institutional character is captured by these tendencies (as it always has been) then and to that extent it becomes incapable of doing justice to its own witness to the liberty of God.

That is to say, briefly, that the church can always betray its own symbolic character. The symbol, however, cannot betray itself. A symbol cannot take up a rigid, self-defensive stance. A symbol is not able to impose a message or a programme; it can only offer whatever it has to communicate. A symbol has no social power except the resonance that it excites in the lives of those who respond to it. That is why it is peculiarly appropriate that the gospel of God's love should take institutional form in a complex of symbols, and properly speaking nothing more than that. Love requires language, and language is itself a social institution. But love imposes nothing, and the language used by love has to work in a way that elicits a sense of love, calls for it, draws it out, and gives people courage to speak it themselves. That is to say it has to work symbolically, as a means by which the courage to be free for love is communicated among men and women and established within them.

Christian faith and Christian hope look forward to a moment when form and freedom will coincide in total knowledge, when we shall see God face to face and know as we are known. But that coincidence of form and freedom is also (in one vital way) possible now to the church and to the believer, not in power relationships or in practical achievements, but in *sign*. The church lives by signs, signs which point at one and the same time to the open truth and to the inexhaustible mystery of God's love. The church is also called to be such a sign itself. Ultimately that is the only sufficient justification for its institutional existence. However, lest anyone should think this is a weak admission, arrived at only grudgingly, we must insist that the justification *is* sufficient – totally sufficient.

CHAPTER FIVE

Priesthood, Symbol and Doctrine

> The cult-man stands alone in Pellam's land: more precariously than he knows he guards the *signa*: the pontifex among his house-treasures, (the twin-*urbes* his house is) he can fetch things new and old: the tokens, the matrices, the institutes, the ancilia, the fertile ashes – the palladic foreshadowings: the things come down from heaven together with the kept memorials, the things lifted up and the venerated trinkets.
>
> David Jones, *The Anathemata*

1. The Ministries 'of Angels and Men'

Older readers may be familiar with a prayer for the clergy which begins like this:

> O God, who art ever adored by the holy angels,
> yet dost choose men to be the stewards of thy mysteries . . .

Behind the manner of this address lies, presumably, the way the epistle to the Hebrews compares God's use of the angels with his choice of humankind in Christ. 'He took not angels but the seed of Abraham' (Heb. 2.16). But the prayer proposes, what Hebrews never did, an alternative scheme for the ministry of the church. We are not meant to take this scheme seriously, but suppose we at least entertained it further before dismissing it – what then? What would it mean if angels, not humans, were ministers of God's church and stewards of his mysteries?

We should not expect the angels to appear in more or less human guise and do the things the existing clergy do. The idea of angels as counterfeit humans reminds us forcibly that, in the ministry, we are already inclined to treat humans as counterfeit angels. The clergy present an appearance of common humanity, but are also often expected to collude with its denial. How much difference would it really make for the perception of priesthood as a godlike, separated occupation, if priests really did descend into their parsonages from somewhere beyond, with no previous experience of human life, no anxieties of their own, no sexuality, no political commitments, no need for recreation – nothing but untroubled authority and an inexhaustible capability to be agreeable?

We might have that if we really wanted it without putting angels to the trouble. No, if angels are to be conceived of as attending to the mysteries of God they must do it from heaven, where they belong, even though the mysteries are to be encountered on earth. We have already imagined that the church has to operate as a system of symbols. Let us simply give that system up into the care of angels. Its workability will not depend – again, we have already said it – on organised programmes and cunningly devised arguments. It will depend on the power of the symbols themselves and on the way people intuitively and inevitably turn to them as markers of decisive truth in their lives. And angels can at least be trusted to ensure that symbols have power, and that they turn up at the right moments in the lives of men and women. Much of the time they need come only to the attention of individuals, the way poetic images touch the minds only of those who read the poems, however universal in their appeal. But it could be that their universal, public quality would actually draw people together from time to time to celebrate them. Essentially this coming together would happen spontaneously, even if once in a while an organising committee had to be formed. People would gather to do what people do when they are most themselves, and most at home with one another. The whole of human culture (for what or who could be excluded?) might come out looking like 'The Lore and Language of School Children'[1] – a system of rhymes and pass-words, games and rigmaroles, badges of identity and seasonal observances which really would be more caught than taught, and when it is taught, taught by no one in particular, just whoever happens to know.

Now it appears that a good deal of religion is like this – implicit or 'natural' religion. There are symbols which recur again and again in human culture, offering a sense of meaning, covering over the abrasions of life with an ointment compounded of mystery and inevitability. And the system which such symbols make up has authority. You cannot quarrel with the naturalness of nature. If any change is to happen it could happen only through the (not impossible) change of nature itself and its consequent effect on human sensibility.

Perhaps this is what angelically mediated religion really would be, or is. 'Holy, holy, holy is the Lord of hosts; the whole earth is full of his glory.' *Is* full – not could or might or will be, but simply *is*. 'Nature as nature is' has its worship, which is simply to be itself. Those mighty powers of being which need no redemption because they have never fallen from their true nature would seem to be the ideal ministers of such a cult.

But a religion of redemption cannot be like that. The very idea of redemption implies that nature is no longer itself, that its appearance must be questioned, its future proclaimed as something different from its present. A redemptive action must, to be redemptive, stand out from the rest of experience, distinct and discontinuous. It calls for novel judgements, changes of mind, pursuits of understanding. It offers positive truths to those who believe, which may be truthfully received, or may be distorted in the receiving. With redemptive religion comes the possibility of heresy. How would the angels handle heresy? Can we imagine them holding a celestial Nicene council to discuss the serious mutation of redemption-lore that has occurred in Alexandria? What kind of angelic power over human minds and hearts would be needed to correct such an aberration?

All of which shows that God chose humanity to be the steward of his mysteries from the moment that he chose us at all, from the moment he proposed to create a being whose freedom would answer to his own. Somehow – there is no escaping it – human beings have to take it upon themselves to guard and keep, to present and interpret the symbolic images which articulate God's way with us. We have to judge for ourselves what the truth of God is for us – not, of course, apart from revelatory events or the guiding of the Holy Spirit. Yet even there we have to judge what events are really revelatory and what movements in the human spirit are really movements of the Spirit of God. There can be no escape from personal responsibility in our dealings with God. That is why no revelation can be received passively, without either repentance or fresh hope, and why revelatory events must include the faith-response of those who share in them. That is why in the end God can only be shown forth in a human life, as in Christ, and Christ can only be shown forth in a human society, the church.

Considerations like these must greatly affect the way we think of Christian doctrine. Here we are concerned with one of the most intimate aspects of the problem. What does it mean for the particular people in question that God chooses humans to be the stewards of his mysteries? What does it mean to be the guardian, bearer and interpreter of the symbol of Christ?

Certainly it cannot mean anything less than to be engaged by God at the very deepest level of one's own personality. A priest or a corporate priesthood is never an actor playing a part which could, at least in principle, be separated from the personalities involved. The symbolic form of Christ cannot be put on like a dramatic mask, still less projected onto a screen from a mechanical projector which just happens to need an operator – no matter who. When the priest sets forth Christ he or she has nowhere to hide.

It would take away some embarrassment here if we did not have to speak of 'the priest' in the singular. We could recognise the fact that the Christian priesthood is a genuinely corporate affair, involving different kinds of vocation which are not to be reduced to a single model. It would allow us to avoid the question, which inclusive language has not yet answered, of the singular personal pronoun.

But the idea of an individual priest is unavoidable because priesthood is never independent of personality. However much we conceive of ministry as a distribution of gifts within the one body, it is also the manifestation of the Holy Spirit's action within each individual concerned. However much the ministry takes place within a corporate context, supported by the ministries of other Christians, it remains that the truth which God commits to a minister has to be answered by the minister's own personal truth. Responsibility in public things can be shared in the sense of divided or duplicated, and in that sense the individual burden can be reduced. But the responsibility I bear before God for my own conscience, my own response to his grace, cannot be diminished. This is an essential element in any true ministry or priesthood. Perhaps St John's image of the Good Shepherd can be given this significance too, beyond any special meaning it has in St John's scheme of images, that it shows that good shepherding can only be fully achieved by a single, rounded person who can take responsibility for his or her own life and who therefore has power to lay it down.

Priesthood then is something that claims the whole person. This comes over very clearly in the way the liturgical duties of a priest are never merely ceremonial, and never find their terminus within the liturgy. Priests' liturgical actions hand them over, one way or another, to those they act for and to their concerns. Strangely this fact may be nearer general recognition because of the way lay people are increasingly given distinct, individual roles to play in the liturgy of the church. These people find themselves bound in a new way to their fellow worshippers and to all mankind. You cannot minister the chalice to people and yet remain indifferent to them. You cannot lead intercessions for people in church and close your heart to them in the world. Things of this kind point to that union of the priestly and pastoral character which has always been present in Christian ministry.[2] So the actions of the one who presides at the eucharist, stretching out hands over the church's offerings, establish or re-establish a deeply rooted pastoral relationship with the rest of the church. Typically that would mean between him or her and the congregation he or she leads. In the modern church, with its complex adaptation to modern society, that simple 'community model' of priesthood is not always appropriate. Nevertheless in some way or other the pastoral consequences of the exercise of priesthood ought to be worked out. The sacraments that a priest administers to people that he or she cannot meet in any other way remain (for him or her) frustrated sacraments because they seem to pledge a care, a practical love, which he or she cannot in fact follow through. No doubt the credit can be transferred, but there should be no doubt that the debt exists.

2. The Symbol of Love

If the character of priesthood is such that the priest is engaged as a person to the things which priestly action symbolises, then it is necessary that we look further into the question of what a symbol is.[3] A useful approach is provided by Christopher Bryant, who says, 'A living symbol might be explained as a powerful image, focussing the imagination, releasing the emotions, moving to action.'[4] This is to define the notion of symbol in terms of the way symbols work upon those who receive them. If nothing works and nothing happens there is no symbol. Whatever objective form they may take, symbols have to operate as determinants of human behaviour, and as giving shape to human consciousness. That is how they demonstrate their symbolic character.

Bryant is speaking of symbols from a psychological perspective. According to his Jungian approach symbolic images unify the personality because they enable the calculating ego to get in touch with the subconscious where the power of the symbol really finds its answer. In this way the personality is unified around an action to which the whole person is truly committed. A symbol, then, is a symbol for me insofar as it enables me to act in harmony with myself, to commit myself reasonably yet beyond the calculations of reason, and with the full cooperation of my emotional drives.

But the same idea of a unifying symbol could be given a social application. We could say that something has symbolic power insofar as it focusses the public imagination and so unites the sentiments and actions of individuals with those of other people. When people are set together before a symbol which they all respond to, they discover that they hold certain intuitive judgements in common, share certain priorities and respond in concert with one another to certain events. Such public solidarity, rooted in symbolic awareness, can be observed in the fields of politics and commerce, as much as in religion. Wherever public opinion achieves some measure of active agreement, and the rightness of this agreement is felt to be self-evident, we can take it that the power of a public symbol is at work. Now these things may sound sinister because the examples that spring most readily to mind are indeed sinister – the apparatus of Nazi propaganda focussed on the symbol of the *führer*, the hate-symbols that direct the emotions of a people at war, or the images and slogans of advertising that might appear trivial if they did not focus an unreflective commitment to a selfish way of life. Yet abuse does not take away use, and no people lives as a people, no group can sustain its own emotional solidarity, without a system of symbols which 'focus the imagination, release the emotions and move it to action.' As the actions of social groups are seldom simple and often extremely complex we may suppose that the stock of symbols which each group holds in common is wonderfully rich and varied. Nevertheless, certain symbolic images are likely to be dominant within it, and what these are affects the character of the group at a very deep level.

Public symbols get themselves noticed and reflected on most often when the behaviour they inspire is eruptive, sudden in its impact. But public symbols can also have a conservative, stabilising effect and then they are much less noticeable. Then we are resting upon them, not reacting to them. We have a symbolic picture of the world as we imagine it to be, and as long as the real world shows itself to us as a plausible likeness of that symbolic picture we are at peace. Our cosmic anxiety is not aroused, and we are not disposed to question anything.

All the same it may seem that when public symbols are not moving us to eruptions of greed and anger they are sustaining nothing better than pride and complacency. If that were the limit of their potential the only possible Christian attitude to them would be a total iconoclasm. Images would have to be destroyed, not only in the market and the church but in literature and song, in speech and in thought. If our human capacity for symbols simply locks us up in our own self-enclosed world and makes us the victim of our own self-regard, public symbols must be condemned as the enemies of human dignity. And yet it appears that without the language of symbols, by which we can articulate our own self-transcendence, we humans are not ourselves. That being so we have to look beyond the purposes for which symbolic universes are normally evolved – to establish power, discourage questioning, and foster complacency – and ask whether public symbols can actually sustain freedom. If they cannot, then a Christian religion is an impossibility. But if such matters as freedom, repentance and genuine hope can be made articulate through symbols then a Christian religion is not merely possible, it is necessary.

Symbols, to be Christian, must be able to disclose a judgement and a grace – specifically the judgement and the grace of God. They must speak to men and women of that which comes to them from beyond themselves and so redeems them.

Now we have already argued that, according to one meaning of the phrase, all symbols point 'beyond themselves'. The symbolic image or phantasy may be quite simple – an apple, a sword, an attractive man or woman or an unattractive beast – but that which it symbolises is far from simple. What is symbolised is a complex of memories, associations, trained responses – probably ambiguous to reason and certainly beyond intellectual analysis. Symbols have a kind of transcendental intentionality, by the way they refer to mysteries rather than to objects. The symbol may be perceived as the image of an object, but it represents a mystery which is not reducible to something merely objective.

Yet once that point of discrimination has been reached it is actually easier to see what the symbolic image and the mystery it symbolises have in common than to separate them. Conventional signs are distinguished from real symbols in that real symbols participate in the mystery they symbolise.[5] When we touch them we are in touch with the mystery, because the mystery is present and active in them. But, if we are looking for a way in which God's dealings with humanity can be symbolised, this is not enough. Again we must say this arises from the way God has created men and women in real freedom, real independence from himself. There is a created separability of God and humanity which is God's own gift to us. Human culture, with all its moral ambiguities, is one of the consequences of that gift. If then God in his redemptive grace is to be symbolised within human culture the symbols employed must have a very special transcendent reference. They must point 'beyond' in the sense of 'away from' themselves. They must not point into their own depths, which would only be the depths of the culture of which they were part. They must, as it were, cancel themselves out in order to give place to God, calling out with whatever voice they have '*non nobis Domine* – not unto us, O Lord, but unto thy name!'

A familiar example of such a symbol is found in the writings of Julian of Norwich.[6]

> Also in this he shewed a little thing, the size of a hazel-nut, which seemed to lie in the palm of my hand; and it was as round as any ball. I looked upon it with the eye of my understanding, and thought, 'What may this be?' I was answered in a general way, thus: 'It is all that is made.' I wondered how long it could last; for it seemed as though it might suddenly fade away to nothing, it was so small. And I was answered in my understanding: 'It lasts, and ever shall last: for God loveth it. And even so hath everything being – by the love of God.'

Cancellation is a feature of this symbol from the moment it appears. What comes to mind is the image of a hazelnut, round as a ball, in the palm of a hand. The fact that Julian said that she saw, not a hazelnut, but something like it, does not destroy the image – we still think of a hazelnut – but it does negate it. Her words allow the image to stand and yet call for its cancellation at the same time. The same union of positive image and negative intention is then found in the way the little round thing like a nut is regarded – not for its roundness or nuttiness but for its littleness, a littleness near to nothingness and actually evoking nothingness. Yet that in turn evokes something which cannot be represented directly at all, but which is actually the positive content of the symbol, the love of God by which all things are sustained.

Two features of Julian's exposition are important here, and may be looked for wherever this kind of symbolism is at work. First, the symbol needs to be taken in a special way, which is actually odd and contrary to common sense. The nut is there, but we must conceive it as not there. It has to evoke an intuition of being and non-being[7] if it is to work as it does for Julian. It has to say, not, see what I am, but, see what I am not. Secondly, to be taken in this special way it must be presented appropriately. Somehow those who give their attention to the symbol have to be guided into sustaining that attention in a paradoxical way. There would seem to be no question of the image of the nut commanding this paradoxical transformation by itself. Julian, as presenter of the symbol, is essential to the symbol's working.

The case is different, in at least one respect, when the symbolic image is not a thing but a person, for here the presenter and the matter presented can be one. The negative, cancelling action then is not imposed secondarily upon the image from outside but is accepted and declared from within the image itself. For a Christian the supreme instance of this must be the person of Christ crucified. The cross, or more exactly the one who dies on the cross, is a real symbol of divine love. God's love is present and perceptible in the death of Christ (Rom. 5.8). Yet some discrimination is needed if we are to say how this symbol presents itself. Is it that the love of Christ himself is fully manifested in it – his own divinity being assumed – or is it that his own human reliance on the love of God is fully tested here and so, having passed the test, becomes a permanent testimony to that love. I think we have to say that the first line of argument, though orthodox and even scriptural (Gal. 2.20), really takes a short cut to a declaration that ought to be approached in the manner of the second. Christ attests the love of the Father by his total commitment to whatever the Father wills. He allows himself to be cancelled out, as the bearer of the symbol of God's truth, not only physically in his dying, but also in his disposition towards himself and others. He does not thrust his suffering in the face of an unloving humanity, demanding an answering love in return. Rather he points to a love which both he and all humanity can trust absolutely.

Yet, of course, once this point is recognised, there is nothing to prevent us speaking of the love of Christ, and entrusting ourselves to that. He has become the definition of God's love. Here at least the presenter cannot be separated from what he presents – a love in which there is no self-assertion.

3. Ministry as the Carrier of Doctrine

The only really serious doctrinal question about the Christian ministry is whether in its very existence it proclaims the doctrine of the cross. This proclamation must not be merely accidental, as when a friend of mine takes the opportunity to remind me of the cross, though he would be my friend even if he didn't. The ministry must proclaim the cross by what it is as well as by what – in an additional effort to justify itself – it does. The question is whether that is possible. Can a human structural institution actually take the stuff of human life and root it in Christ crucified? Can an organised system of symbol-bearing human beings show forth the cross? Will not the fact of organisation itself come into conflict with the symbolic meaning it is supposed to bear?

Our answer so far is that in theory this is possible. The nature of symbols is such that they can, by a kind of permanent self-cancellation, point to the reality of Christ's self-emptying. The nature of institutional structure is such that it can exist for the sake of anti-structure. The question now is a more historical and concrete one – has this happened and does it happen in practice? Does the Christian ministry as it has actually evolved witness to the cross?

If that is the question, and the only real question, a certain approach to Christian ministry is excluded from the start. People would like to believe that somewhere outside the church and its ministry God has declared his antecedent will, and the business of church and ministry is to conform to it. If not on tablets of stone, then at least on something analogous to a book of directions handed down from on high it ought to be possible to read what form the ministry is to take, what powers it is to exercise, what duties it is to perform, and who, in particular, is to be deemed a member of it. Now it is not that these questions ought not to be asked. If we are dealing with an institution, we must be able to describe it in institutional terminology. What is objectionable here is the idea that God has provided the answer to these questions in a way which is logically prior to the existence of the institution itself. If this were the case then the ministry, far from bringing its members into conformity to the cross, would set them at the most remote distance from it. It would provide them with an institutionalised security founded upon the most solid guarantees imaginable.

Textbook treatments of Christian doctrine usually deal with the ministry towards the end of what they say. That in itself suggests that the ministry is secondary upon other matters – such as relate to the canon of scripture, or the doctrines of the creed. What is more, the style of argument normally has to change at that point, because the kinds of argument that trace the forms of dogma back to the event of Christ can no longer be made to work when it comes to the shape of the ministry. Nevertheless, the sense that the ministry is not doctrinally indifferent is a proper one. The ministry has as much practical effect as the scripture and the creeds on the way Christian doctrine is perceived and lived. If it did not in fact communicate the same faith though in another medium this would be a disaster for the faith.

One feature at least which the scriptures, the doctrines of the creeds and the ministry have in common is that all these are given with the church itself; none is imposed upon the church from beyond. As a matter of history it is clear enough that the canon of scripture, the creeds and the formal institution of the ministry all evolved in the church during the same period. But that is no mere contingency. The church's doctrinal task, which is inseparable from its existence, had to be carried out through historical evolution. No other way was possible. And this task extended beyond the evolution of the obviously doctrinal institutions – scripture and creeds – to the ministry as well. It would not be tolerable if the shape the ministry took was contradictory to the faith as it had come to be stated in doctrine.

Creed and scriptures were not handed down from outside the church, but neither did the church invent them, except, if we like, in that primitive sense of invention which means uncovering. The elements which make up the creeds and the scriptures were found to be present within the church's life. Their authority was recognised and, around that recognition, they coalesced and were distinguished. The church did not bestow authority upon these things, even though they had all and severally been composed by the church's members, but it recognised them as God's gifts, as tokens of the grace which had called it into being.

How was that recognition made? The quick answer – through the Holy Spirit – is too quick here. Looking at the experience itself, without doctrinal interpretation, we must say that it was made through a shared sense that it had to be done, a sense rooted in common discourse and worship, nurtured by the shared experience of faith. If the church were able to recognise the word of God in these things it could only be because these things elicited and satisfied its own readiness to hear that word. And if the church is not in fact to be regulated from outside its own membership then perception of this kind, however precarious, must be allowed to arise within the church, and the church must be allowed to draw out and objectify its own tacit awareness of what God is doing within it. The answer to the question, What is the church? must be given with the church itself. It cannot enter the church by any other means. The confession which links belief 'in the Holy Spirit' to belief 'in the Holy Church,' testifies precisely to this – that God's own criterion of Christian truth is given within Christian experience and cannot be sought outside it.

So with the ministry. The question, What is the ministry within the church? can only be answered within the experience of the ministry. The same tacit sense of what it is we are about, or rather what God is about with us, must be allowed its force here too.

That does not mean that the ministry simply imposes itself as a brute fact, not to be understood by the believing mind, not subject to the critique of Christian faith. Quite the contrary. Because the faith that acknowledges the authority of scripture and creed is the same as that which acknowledges the authority of the ministry, we have to look for some necessary congruence between these relatively independent institutions. Those who, in faith, search the scriptures and confess the creeds also work with the ministry and even enter it. One faith is active in all these actions. The ministry, too, then, must be a declaration of that faith.

Perhaps it worked like this. The first-century church gave itself to a great variety of experiments in ministry. In the second century it might have gone further, as each half-formed experience was taken to its various possible conclusions. In fact there was a convergence, a simplification, and a universalising of those elements that were to last. Again, judging the experience for itself, many things could account for this. Historical contingencies would give certain tendencies an opening and close the door on others. The symbolic imagination, which always likes to unite as many perceptions as possible in a single statement, would work in the church toward a structure of ministry which was plainer in design, richer in significance. The theological and moral conscience of Christians would rule out certain developments as not really true to Christian sensibility, while others would be promoted because they drew attention to questions of principle and also answered them satisfactorily. Behind all this would be the conviction, not necessarily explicit, that Christian life, worship and organisation make a statement about Christian faith that is not essentially different from the statement made in Christian doctrinal institutions. So the ministry would be, and would have to be, conformed to Christian doctrine and would become a carrier of doctrine.

Now it is this body of doctrine which the ministry carries in its institutional form that is the 'doctrine of the ministry'. It is not a special doctrine, in which the ministry figures as a special item of faith, or which requires a ministry to be established in conformity with itself. It is ordinary Christian teaching and understanding of what Christian life is about, but embodied in the forms which Christian ministry takes. Perhaps the best way of seeing how this works is to see what scope it offers for change. At any moment in history the ministry will have a, probably rather complex, given form. There will be articulate convictions about it, and other questions which are less certainly answered, but where uncertainty is tolerable. If a conviction is challenged, or a clarification of uncertainty is proposed, then, along with all the practical considerations that may be advanced, the matter must be tested doctrinally. In what way is the faith itself at stake here? If a principle of faith is likely to be obscured or contradicted, just so far the church is warned against the change. But if a prospective change offers an enhanced perception of faith – as may well be possible in a changing world – just so far the church should be encouraged to pursue it.[8]

In the end, all such questions lead back to the cross. The issue is whether the ministry is to become a system of unambiguous self-assertion for its members and for the church whose ministry it is or whether, symbolically and practically, it delivers them over into God's hands. We have to say 'unambiguous' because institutional self-assertion in some form cannot be avoided, but it can be institutionally contradicted in the place where it appears. St Paul knew perfectly well that Christ's ministers would preach themselves, however foolishly proud such preaching might be, but as long as their preaching was directed to Christ he could say 'We preach not ourselves but Christ Jesus as Lord and (only then do we preach) ourselves your servants for Jesus' sake' (2 Cor. 4.5).

CHAPTER SIX

The Living Symbol

> This priesthood . . . is the office which ritually, inwardly and ascetically shares in the dying and rising of Christ.
>
> Ulrich Simon, *A Theology of Auschwitz*

1. The Symbolic Form of the Ministry

So we turn to the living symbol itself, to the typical forms and actions of the Church's inherited ministry. How do these forms bear witness to the gospel, what Christian doctrines do they carry? But first, let us remind ourselves of what is already established, and what remains to be tested.

(a) Consecratory Intention

Christian priesthood must conform symbolically to the cross and point beyond itself. This implies a self to point beyond – the individual self of the priest and further, the social self of the institution. Consecration to God does not give meaning to an object or action for the first time. Rather it takes an earlier natural and social meaning, acknowledges it and then transcends it. The eucharistic bread has first of all the symbolic value of bread itself – 'which earth has given and human hands have made' – before it becomes 'for us, the Bread of Life'. It is natural and cultural – the two taken together in Christian thought, though anthropology tends to divide them – before it is spiritual. There is a selfhood in human institutions which reaches up from the most elemental level to the richest enjoyments of human society, and the act of consecration affirms this at the same time that it lays the matter open in a new way to the glory of God.

In G. M. Hopkins' sonnet, 'Kingfishers catch fire', he takes up the theme of a scholastic axiom and then goes beyond it. *Operatio sequitur esse* – as a thing is, so it acts,[1] but at the human level we can go beyond this. By grace the human self is made transparent to the divine.

As Kingfishers catch fire, dragonflies draw flame;
As tumbled over rim in roundy wells
Stones ring; like each tucked string tells, each hung bell's
Bow swing finds tongue to fling out broad its name;
Each mortal thing does one thing and the same:
Deals out that being indoors each one dwells;
Selves – goes itself; *myself* it speaks and spells,
Crying *What I do is me: for that I came.*
I say more: the just man justices;
Keeps grace: that keeps all his goings graces;
Acts in God's eye what in God's eye he is –
Christ – for Christ plays in ten thousand places,
Lovely in limbs, and lovely in eyes not his
To the Father through the features of men's faces.

Grace is the key word, here. When grace is 'kept' – recognised, received and lived – then nature as the proclamation of nature's self is converted to the proclamation of God's glory. Natural and cultural symbols are not alien to God but they still have to be appropriated to him, their strength set alongside his strength, and so called completely into question. The fact that they endure in the presence of God has to be seen as his gift. When men and women recognise that this is true for themselves they are led to a response of self-denial, self-consecration. 'I live', says Paul, 'yet not I. Christ lives in me' (Gal. 2.20). Affirmation and negation coincide here, in a coincidence we have to look for in every symbol of the gospel. The message by itself, that we find ourselves only by losing ourselves in Christ, is not enough. The gospel ministry must be possessed by that message as its own intrinsic form.

(b) Human Beings as Symbols

A symbol becomes socially effective only if it shapes and energises the external acts, the social relationships and the inward dispositions of men and women. Priesthood happens whenever certain people accept the task consciously of enabling this to happen. Inevitably this is a matter of some complexity. Symbolic value is found in people in many different ways, and the responses it evokes have all kinds of social ramifications. Some sort of system can be postulated or it will not all hold together, but it will be a marvellously variegated system in itself. In a morality play a character may 'symbolise' a divine energy or a virtue in an imposed, one-dimensional way. In real life symbolic forms are much more subtly informative of thought and action, conscience and feeling. In the case of the Christian priesthood we can look for symbolic meaning in several spheres and kinds of action.

(i) *In the way people enter the priesthood; in ordination.*
(ii) *In the way the church organises itself around the functions of its ministers.*
(iii) *In the way ministers at the liturgy are themselves part of the liturgy's symbolic system.*
(iv) *In the way this liturgical function spills over into the rest of community life and culture.*
(v) *In individual encounters, when someone looks for the gifts of God through the ministry of the priest.*
(vi) *In the personal imagination of priests, respecting their own identity and meaning as human beings, and so in their moral conduct and in their prayer.*

If we follow up these clues we can at least begin to answer the question, 'How are priests related to the symbolism of God's grace?' They may at certain points be objectively identified with it. They may awaken a sense of grace in others. They may join with others in the celebration of God's grace, in a manner that requires the presence of both. They may perceive it as a claim upon themselves, judging and rescuing them. We are dealing here with a complex of social and individual experiences, of outward signs and inward motives. We are not dealing with something reducible to a simple claim that can be simply established or refuted.

There is a claim, however, and it can be tested.

(c) Doctrinal Congruence

I want to take the suggestion further now, that the ministry of the church carries certain doctrines, that in its structure and action it is an embodiment of those doctrines. I want to say that its congruence in this way with Christian doctrine is the only real test of truth or distortion in its practice, the only real justification for its existence. Does the doctrinal system which takes concrete form in the ministerial structure of the church really represent Christ or not? If we analyse the structure, certain key doctrinal ideas that support and maintain it appear. We need to clarify these ideas, at the same time perceiving how, within the mutual relationships that make up the church, they lay claim to the lives of Christians, and so manifest themselves as a living symbol. We shall have to ask whether the forms of doctrine which are published in this way are in accord with other, scriptural and dogmatic forms. We need to test both their theoretical and practical meaning against the ascetical principle that, through them, human life is made subject to the grace and judgement of the cross. It is through the union of these factors that the evident Christianity of the priesthood will appear if it appears at all.

2. The Representation of God in Christ

'Priests act in the person of Christ the Head.'[2] That representative function of the church's ministers is most evident in the liturgy – in their presidency at the eucharist, in absolution, in the highly significant even if theologically imprecise action of blessing. It is also implicitly present in all their pastoral relationships. Priests are perceived as people who respect the confidence of those who speak to them, not merely because professional ethics require it but because such confidences are made, in a spirit of faith, not to them personally but to God.

Of course the general sociological category of 'religious functionary' might be used to account for most or all of this, but for Christian faith this generalising approach has to be qualified if not denied. For the Christian, making use of a priest's ministry, that priest is the representative of Christ. That representation takes the form of religious function, it affirms and makes use of the social necessity of priesthood, but the theological truth is primary. God in Christ can be represented by human beings – that is, by the church and in the church.

All kinds of objections may be raised to this blunt assertion and we can allow ourselves a useful parenthesis here to look at the most serious of them, the moral one. How can the manipulative, divisive, unloving and violent actions of the church down the ages be seen as the deeds of representatives of Christ? How can the social and psychological terror, that the churches have so often sought to defend, be understood except as a refutation of the claim to represent Christ? There is no reflection of the image of the Lord here but only contradiction. And, so far as the church accepts the standpoint from which the accusation is made, it cannot respond to it except with a plea of guilty. Yet the church in making this plea goes outside itself. Within itself it knows what God has done with human guilt. If objectors can be led to come inside, to join the Christian in admitting their own sin and in looking to Christ not for approval but for pardon, they can find another perspective on the matter. If people want to criticise the church and do it in the name of humanity then the only responsible arguments they can bring are moral ones. Other arguments say only that the church has rivals. But the church concedes the moralist's case. It knows it has not lived up to its calling. Still though, it also knows the gift of repentance and the grace of forgiveness. It sees its Lord in a way that the moralist does not, and in that perspective it is called to represent him. And to tell the truth the moralist does not reject the idea of representation, but accepts it, only to misunderstand and so mis-apply it.

In the gospels the representative quality of certain people seems to have little to do with their moral character. It is rather that they are, in a peculiar and disturbing way, available. They invite us, against some of our inclinations, to receive them. In all the gospels there occurs a pattern of words which we can call 'the double reception formula'. It is given more than one application, and it is expanded in different ways, but the key idea is the same in each case. It is that God himself is received by those who receive Jesus, and that Jesus in turn is received when certain other designated people are received.

In Matthew's gospel, when Jesus sends out the twelve as preachers of the Kingdom he says to them, 'He who receives you receives me, and he that receives me receives him who sent me' (Matt. 10.40). Nothing less is at stake here than the mission of the Christ himself, the validity of his claim to reveal the Father and to make God known to mankind. If Jesus is not himself the one sent by God then his own sending of the apostles is empty of meaning and authority. Here then the reception formula articulates the awareness of an apostolic church that its faith in Jesus and its own *raison d'être* are entirely bound up together. Jesus represents God as one sent by him, and the church represents Jesus because he in turn has sent it into the world. The crux of the matter is whether people in the world can recognise the apostolic, representative character of the church. If they can, and if they respond to it, then the church's spokesmen 'count as' Jesus himself for them, just as Jesus himself 'counts as' God.

Luke uses the formula in a very similar context, but with an interesting variation. The single expectation that some people will receive the messengers of Christ is expanded into two stark alternatives – that they should be 'heard' or 'rejected' (Luke 10.16). To speak of being heard is to tie the formula even more firmly to the church's awareness of itself as a body sent with a message, a proclamation. To speak of being rejected is to remind the church that its mission from Christ brings it into historical conformity with him. The church is not free to stand apart from the message it bears. As God's mission works itself out through Christ and then through the church, the church is called into functional identity with Christ. It has to bear the pain of its apostolic calling in its own body.

But then there is another application of the reception formula, and a group of related sayings, which seem to point in quite another direction. An incident common to all three synoptic gospels, though with variations, has Jesus respond to the question, 'Who is the greatest?' by taking a child, and by saying (according to Mark's version), 'Whosoever shall receive one of such little children in my name receives me, and whoever receives me receives not me but him who sent me' (Mark 9.37). Here, in spite of the qualifying phrase 'in my name', it is something intrinsic to childhood which makes the child a functional representative of Christ. Similarly in the Matthean parable of judgement, the punch line 'inasmuch as you did it for the most humble of these my brethren you did it for me' (Matt. 25.40) is meant to draw attention to the humiliation and destitution which bring 'the brethren' into conformity and identity with Christ. We seem to be faced here with a stark polarity of choice. The reception formula can be so applied as to mean that God in Jesus is represented in those who speak for him, his apostolic messengers, or it can be applied to mean that he is represented in the 'little ones', in the poor, the hungry and thirsty, and in children. But can it possibly be both?[3]

The apostolic church seems to have had its own doubts on this matter, which is why it is not just children but 'children in my name' who have to be received, and why the question arises, in connection with these and certain other texts, whether the terms 'the poor' and 'little ones' are not metaphorical equivalents for 'disciples'. Is it really the poor as poor who are designated Christ's 'brethren' in the parable of judgement, or is it that they are already Christ's 'brethren' for some other reason – as members of the church, perhaps – and their poverty lays them open to a certain kind of recognition by the world? That interpretation seems to be borne out by the Matthean saying, 'Whoever will give one of these little ones a cup of cold water to drink in the name of (that is, because he or she is) a disciple shall in no way lose his reward' (Matt. 10.42).

All the same, it is disciples in their poverty and thirst, not in riches and power, who elicit the unwitting perception of Christ in them from their fellow men. Christ identifies himself with the disciples, and he identifies himself with the poor, and however closely we bring these two acts of identification together, they remain distinct in principle, and therefore all the more illuminating when they are joined.

Unlike the disciples the poor are not *assumed* into identity with the Son of Man: he recognises himself in them and places himself among them. It is people like them, who have no stake in the world's possessions and who live by grace alone, who are to be recognised without further ado as the bearers of God's cause. The Kingdom of God belongs to them. Christ's mission finds its goal in them. Their disposition before God which, if they take God seriously at all, can only be one of longing and readiness for grace, sets the pattern for any ministry which takes Christ's name.

Yet Christ's identity with the poor does not comprehend his significance so fully that only such things as are done for them count as done for him. He also maintains his own identity, and his own distinctive office, as the one sent by the Father to make the Father known (Matt. 11.27). Can he, in that office, be truly represented by other human beings? The testimony of the gospels is that he can, provided he himself calls and commissions them. Whereas the poor are identified with Christ from the beginning, the apostolic ministers of Christ are chosen. They are taken into his confidence and given a particular, personal part in his mission. Their identity with him is more than a fact. It is a gift and a charge.

John too makes use of the double reception formula. The ambiguity of the synoptic uses has its origin in two aspects of Jesus' own behaviour, his solidarity with the poor and his choice of the twelve, which though connected could not be reduced to one another. John takes up these themes afresh, but in a new and unambiguous synthesis – that of the apostolic and therefore suffering church.

His version of the formula runs: 'He that receives the one I send receives me, and he that receives me receives the one who sent me' (John 13.20). Here the formula has been abstracted from any ambiguous historical situation and set free from any particular historical reference. In receiving this word the apostolic church acknowledges the charge laid upon it by the Son who himself received his apostolic charge from the Father. As the discourse develops it is made clear that this apostolic vocation has profound ascetical and social consequences for those who accept it. Because they abide in Christ, because they are entrusted with his truth and made alive to it through the Paraclete, they must expect to be treated as he was treated (John 15.20). Really they have no option whether to accept or not. The Father has already given them to Jesus (John 17.6). There is nothing at all accidental about the way his mission is extrapolated in theirs – the Father is the source of both. So when Jesus returns to them in his risen life he assumes their acceptance and simply gives them his commission and his Spirit. '"As the Father sent me, even so I send you," and when he had said this he breathed on them' (John 20.21 & 22).

So if it is claimed for the priests of the church today that they are called to represent Christ, just as he represents the Father, that is not a claim foreign to apostolic Christianity. On the contrary it is the apostolic claim itself, which the church in every age is bound to sustain. It is an enormous claim, disturbing to those who bear it and to those who have to receive it alike, and it would not be surprising if people preferred to make it tacitly rather than overtly. Nevertheless the Lord's gift of the Holy Spirit to the church makes the claim inescapable. Christ is to be found and known through us.

But is it only the church's ordained ministers who are intended by that *us*? If the whole church is baptised into Christ, does not every member have a vocation and ministry within the universal priesthood? If we say yes to the last question must we say no to the first?

Perhaps we can formulate the issues here more precisely under three heads.

(i) *Does the universally shared priesthood of the church rule out the distinction between the ministerial priesthood and the laity within it?*

It certainly does not follow logically that this is the case. It would if the word *priest* in Christian use always meant the same thing, but it does not. There is therefore no contradiction in saying that all the baptised share in God's priesthood but that, nevertheless, the priestly church is served by a particular ministerial priesthood.

All the same a less peremptory approach to the question is possible if we admit first that the various uses of the word *priest* are related to one another analogically, and see secondly that the issue is really about the nature of shared grace in the church. If priesthood is a kind of stuff that one can enjoy only by having it in corporal possession, then for some to have it in special measure is for others to be relatively deprived. But the *koinonia* of grace is not like that. Even though the gifts and graces of God are distributed among the members, all have an interest in them and benefit from them (Rom. 12.4). So the church is evangelistic in its evangelists, prophetic in its prophets, wise in its sages, monastic in its monks, committed to the world through its members who live and work in the world; it is a lay church through its lay members, a servant church in those who perform its diaconal ministry, a shepherding church in its pastors and a priestly church in its priests. If it is true that ministerial structure enables the church to find a focus and carrier for the doctrine that God is represented through human beings, then it is totally appropriate that some Christians should exemplify that doctrine in a special way.

(ii) *But are not the distinctions found in the Church really a matter of functional convenience, social rather than theological?*

It seems plausible to say, theologically speaking, that it is the church, the whole church and nothing but the whole church, that represents Christ. We might then say, however, that pragmatic constraints, the demands of efficiency, the impossibility of assembling the whole church, make it necessary to appoint ministers as delegates of that representative authority. In this indirect sense, then, they become Christ's representatives as well. There are various ways of making this pragmatic approach convincing. We can say with Luther that it is neither possible nor becoming for every Christian to carry out the tasks of the ministry. We can reason anthropologically that every society needs a *persona*, a single face in which its group identity is focussed. So, just as the mayor stands for the city, the colonel for the regiment, we can say that the minister stands for the church. Yet to Luther we might put the question, are there not laymen in the church who could perform ministerial functions fittingly and do not? And we could ask the proponents of the anthropological argument whether they are as free from theology as they suppose. There is certainly an analogy to be drawn between the relationship of a church to its pastor and that of a secular institution to its head. But which way round does the analogy work? Is not the natural context for this kind of perception avowedly sacral? People knew about fathers, kings, and priests well before they knew about presidents, chairmen and elected delegates. We see the city imaged forth in the mayor because we are thinking, even if in an attenuated way, about the city as a sacral reality. A genuine corporation always seems to us to be greater and, in some sense, holier than its aggregated members. That is why the functional head of such a corporation can take on a symbolic role as well. He or she carries, in a way no one else does, the odour of its holiness, not only for the world at large but for the members of the corporation itself. Now, apply this to the church and we are back into real theology, for the church desires no 'holiness' but the holiness of God.

(iii) *Is there then a particular theological justification for the existence of the ministerial priesthood?*

Briefly, yes. It is that the church has no holiness, no authority which it can claim as its own and make over to any of its members. It lives before God, always, as a recipient. As John Macquarrie[4] says, it 'has been brought into being from above downwards' and 'this . . . implies the recognition of a relatively independent status belonging to the ordained ministry within the church'. The church would have failed utterly to have recognised its true position of dependence on God if its internal ministries, its preaching, teaching and sacraments, were to be interpreted only as moments in a conversation with itself.[5] The church above all needs to hear its Lord's voice and receive its Lord's gifts, and recognise them as graces it cannot command. So, although the anthropological rationale for the church's ministry is very plausible it leads to a point at which it must itself call for theology. The bishops and priests of the church cannot be merely representatives of the church. They must also be distinctively representatives of Christ. Among the many ministries Christ gives to his apostolic church, they are his apostolic representatives to the church itself. The church cannot consistently commit itself to apostolic mission while forgetting that it needs itself to receive those whom Christ sends it in his own name.[6]

3. Common Membership in the Body

For many centuries, and still perhaps typically, the church assembled for worship was conceived of as a congregation in confrontation with a priest. The duality of priest and laity was an image large enough to explain all situations in church life. Yet classically, and still vestigially, the church's ministerial structure has not been a mere duality but a diversity in unity of at least four orders: laity, deacons, presbyters and bishops. Neither in the liturgy nor in pastoral function are these callings the equivalent of one another, nor is any one sufficient in itself. The action of the eucharist and the practical life of the church require the distinctive contribution which each order brings to it, just as the service each performs looks to the others for its completeness. Ministry is always a matter of mutuality, of initiative and response, of waiting on others and working with others.

Clement of Rome wrote to the Corinthians that Christians should serve God 'each according to his own order'.[7] He argues that any cooperative venture requires differentiation, mutual respect between lesser and greater, and enforces this principle by reference to the coinherence of members in a body – interestingly without acknowledgement to Paul. The institutional structure of the church, for Clement, is at one with its liturgy and its morality. The church's liturgy – really its existence before God – is not constituted by the voluntary action of one or even several people, but only by their entering together upon an order which is given by grace. The liturgy is a symbol of this givenness, a sign to each Christian that, apart from the wholeness of the church, he or she has no standing. And what is true as symbol is true also in organisation, morality, ascetics, in the whole of Christian life. Between the calling of the whole church and that of any individual is the principle of variety in unity. As a Christian I need every other Christian, not merely as an image of myself, an example or a witness to common experience, but in his or her specificity, his or her difference from me. Church life means union through genuine differentiation.

Clement, and the liturgical tradition which follows his principle 'each in his office', clearly differs from Paul in his charismatic interpretation of the image of the body (1 Cor. 12.12ff). Both of course agree that in Christ 'many are one' (1 Cor. 10.17). Christians live as Christians only in the unity which is God's gift and not their own creation. Both teach the need for mutual recognition, respect and love. Nevertheless it would be wrong to try to conflate them or to give one the advantage over the other. It is better to see them as complementary, and as mutual correctives to one another.

What was Paul's basic intention in 1 Corinthians chapters 12 to

14? Why did he raise the question of *pneumatika* – manifestations of spirit – in the life of the church? It was not, as his embarrassed tone shows, to commend them: Corinthian pride in them would make that redundant. It was rather to interpret them, contain them and regulate their use. That is why chapter 13 subordinates *pneumatika* to the more excellent way of love, and the demand at the end of chapter 14 for decency and order must be seen as controlling the whole exposition. But above all Paul sets the entire experience within the theological context of the life of the body. Here pneumatic enthusiasm is made subject to mutual regard, and the pride of power is rebuked. Paul must have exercised his digestion over this matter for some time, for in Romans 12 he returns to the image, though now attempting to apply it with even greater precision. Here the idea of *pneumatika* is discarded, replaced by that of 'the measure of faith' (Rom. 12.3), and Paul goes beyond saying that Christians are 'severally members of the Body of Christ' to saying that they are 'severally members one of another' (Rom. 12.5). Each Christian, then, is a microcosm of the body of Christ, constituted as a Christian by his or her mutual relationship with all other Christians. It is this sense of mutual interdependence which is Paul's major theme in these chapters, and to read them as a commendation of extraordinary powers or as a demand for the sharing out of jobs is far too superficial. The service of God, for Paul, is something to share *in*, a unity constituted by the purpose of God in Christ.

The eucharistic liturgy is a sign of this sharing-in, of mutuality and reciprocity as constitutive of the church. As a sign it does not exhaust the practical possibilities of unifying grace, but it does lay claim to all that the church does, whether charismatically, morally or pragmatically. It enforces the principle. The Corinthians' attachment to *pneumatika* had lent itself to strife and emulation, but it is worth noting that Paul had already detected strife and emulation in the way they conducted themselves at the Lord's Supper, and there the sin was all the more culpable since the sacrament itself proclaimed the unity of the body (1 Cor. 10.15–17). Charismatic enthusiasm carries no sign of its own to counter individual self-centredness, but the sacramental structure of the church points, by its very nature, to self-affirmation only through union with others.

Now it is true that liturgical forms can easily be detached from practical demands. Just because the sacrament manifests the true state of the church it may come to be used as a surrogate for the moral and practical unity which the church ought to have but really lacks. It can be taken as a sign of a perpetually unfulfilled promise. The charismatic stress on the present action of God through the Spirit is a valuable corrective to that, provided it remains itself informed by the summons to unity which the sacrament presents.

In the light of these considerations we have to say that the contemporary church does not stand up well to scrutiny. It is true that much contemporary liturgy is participative in the sense that many people do different things within it. One or two will read, others lead prayers, others again present the offerings or share in the administration of communion, and all this in addition to the traditional tasks of singers, sidesmen, servers, acolytes and so on. That kind of sharing out is meant to put an earlier distortion right, but it corrects it only in part and in other ways only accentuates it. The first distortion was to reduce the plurality of orders in the church's liturgy to a basic duality, of priest and laity. The second was to raise this duality to a state of latent rivalry.

The picture that emerged with the development of low mass as the typical celebration of the eucharist was one in which all liturgical significance was to be found in the priest's action alone; all power rested with him. The liturgy was something he did, and alone could do for others. The church was then perceived as a powerful priesthood ministering to a powerless laity, and the reaction has been to build up a compensating power for the laity as well. This creates a new balance, sometimes in the dangerous sense of an opposition, but it does nothing to correct the original distortion which reduced the church to only two essential functions. The liturgy was once a serious cooperative work bringing together different offices and gifts, each of which had a real pastoral significance. Our attempts to restore that have got no further than a sharing out of little jobs acording to a rota. Everybody gets to do everything some time or other, except what is reserved to the priest. The question then arises from the assumptions already built into the system, why this minimal task ought to be reserved. The proposition is seriously entertained that the common priesthood of the church would be better expressed if the whole congregation were to say the whole eucharistic prayer together, and do without an ordained president.

But the reason why presidency or any other ministry is especially distinguished in church is not that privilege should be denied to others, but that true privilege should be found where alone it can be found in a condition of interdependence. Nor are we to create this condition: it is given and we are called into it. The eucharistic prayer has never been a manifesto, to be read out together, but a dialogue, and in the Orthodox East, where the deacon has a directing function, something richer still. It demands the contribution of diverse gifts, and only so does it achieve unity and universality. Perhaps the confusion of unity with unison proclamation could only occur in a church that had lost its awareness of the trinitarian economy, since it is the doctrine of the Trinity, and the experience which is structured by that doctrine, which establishes it as fundamental for Christians that real unity requires diversity in relationship.

The church then is constituted by its diversity, and in this constitutive function the bishop or the priest who represents the bishop has a vital role to play. When a congregation recognises that it does not constitute a church in itself, as a merely voluntary body, and delivers itself up to the richer unity which the ordained ministry brings to it, it meets the demand that all Christian activity should be founded on a consecratory intention. It is a fairly weak recognition of this principle when the diversity is reduced to a duality, when only the two orders of priest and laity meet in the liturgy. Nevertheless the principle of mutual dependence under God is being acknowledged here, however minimally. If it is true that the laity cannot celebrate without the priest, it is also true that the priest cannot celebrate without the laity. Each waits on the other, and in doing so actually waits upon God.

The priest cannot celebrate without the laity. That needs to be stressed, since some priests overlook it and some deliberately flout it. And if, on exceptional occasions, a priest should legitimately celebrate in solitude, it would be better to see this, not simply as the exercise of a priestly liturgy which he or she ought not be denied, but as the cooperation of that priestly task with the layperson which he or she also is. For really it is not the priest's function which supplies the energy of action, but the layperson's. Alone, and in the specifically priestly role, a priest can do nothing to affect the life of humankind. Liturgical action, preaching, counselling and direction, blessing and absolving, all effect nothing if they do not engage with real human activities. Seen in that way, it is not that priests have power and the laity avail themselves of it, but that the laity have power and that priests bring to it certain consecratory signs. Without the layperson's action the action of the priest is useless.

4. Sacramental Action

A doctrine of the church and of the ministry implies a corresponding doctrine of the way God acts. That kind of question becomes more important the more we dig down beneath the surface behaviour of the church's ministry to ask why it should act as it does. The idea that seems most fitted to answer this question, and to show how the different levels of examination hold together, is that of *sacrament*.

Bishops and the presbyters who act in their name are responsible for the symbolic life of the church, they are symbol-bearers: themselves living symbols. They represent Christ in the church and beyond it. Their order, together with the other orders, is constitutive of the church. Their ministry is committed to a pattern in which the social and natural stuff of human life is both negated so far as its self-possession goes, and taken up into the service of God's grace. They enter upon this ministry by a ritual act of prayer on the part of the church which looks for an answering gift of the Holy Spirit and relies solely upon that. The one idea which unites these different aspects of the church's ministry economically and elegantly is that of God's sacramental action. God is a sacramentally acting God, who therefore creates a sacramental church for himself, and ordains a sacramental ministry within it.

Now it is undoubtedly true that sacramental theology does not take its material primarily from the experience of ministry but from the gospel sacraments of baptism and eucharist, so the question, whether God acts characteristically in a sacramental way, depends on our initial estimate of those two sacraments' place in the purpose of God. It is possible to see the two great sacraments as two ordinances which, so to speak, point to the gospel but form no part of it, two acts which the Lord Jesus instituted in his sovereign freedom, but as only an index to his saving work. If we take this view then we can also take the sign quality and the social aspect of the sacraments as equally accidental, and assume that whatever the Lord does through the sacraments he does in a manner unique to them. Human life and even Christian life can then really go on without them.

But to say this is to say that the most obvious features of the sacraments – their social anthropological functions – are no part of God's intention and no indication of the way God acts in general. It is to say that whatever the sacraments appear to be, they are really something quite different. Such an idea could claim support from both Catholic and Protestant traditions, with their demand that faith should go beyond the outward and visible. Nevertheless, without seeking to eliminate this kind of idea, modern sacramental theology tends to work in the opposite direction, and to see the 'beyond' taking hold of the outward and visible in order to become effectively present to faith. This makes it possible to accept all the features of the sacramental life, even those that seem most compromising and least spiritual, and to ask whether we have not, precisely here, a sign of the way in which the God who loves us actually acts for human salvation. The sacraments are material, and God acts through matter. They are social, and God acts through social institutions. They are symbols, with the manifold valency and inexhaustible depth of symbols, and such symbolic richness is wholly appropriate to God's presentation of himself to us. If these things are not true then the testimony which the sacraments give to their own nature has to be explained away, even and especially at the moments when they are being enacted.

David Jones, who brought to these matters the sensitivity of both a painter and a poet, made much of the eucharist – as the summation of human history and culture, as the cardinal sign around which all human sign-making clustered and found its true form. He quotes Maurice de la Taille on Christ's purpose in the last supper, that 'he placed himself in the order of signs'.[8] Jesus had broken the bread and blessed the cup with the deliberate intention that the medium to which these actions belonged, that of significant ritual, should be his own medium too. By this means he would be found; through these signs he would communicate himself.

God is everywhere active, in the sense that his creative power is present to everything he creates and is manifest in its existence. He is active too in the way his overall provident intention works through each event that occurs, and guides the world gently, with full respect for the nature of things, to its goal in him. This creative and provident action has to be affirmed in any doctrine of God's sacramental action. Nevertheless it has to be said that God's providence is mightily obscure, and that it is his sacramental action which makes it at all comprehensible. The things God has made hide him, rather than display his character and purpose. They do this through their appearance, and even more they do it through their history. Who really can read off the meaning of God's love from the way the world goes? The God who is everywhere at work is nowhere apparent. Even if certain natural beauties, certain historical turns toward the good, seem to us to show his hand at work, we still have to admit that no beauty is permanent and no historical development is unambiguously good. God's action in nature and history is, from a providential point of view, dark, ambiguous, distorted and broken.

What is it then that sustains hope and a sense of direction? The answer lies in the realm of the sacramental, in the order of signs. We do not have to overlook the fact that there are false hopes, just as there are lying signs, to acknowledge that the question of truth or falsehood comes in second here. Primary is the recognition of the medium which has to be consecrated to truth, or given up to falsehood. So it is that, from age to age, and from culture to culture, people perceive the events that disturb or fascinate them most through a system of institutional signs. Birth and marriage, sickness and death, the growing and consumption of food, the defence of the community against attack and subversion, are all surrounded by rituals which carry and sustain a certain interpretation of them. And it is from that interpretation, and the conviction with which it is regularly affirmed, that people take courage to meet life and death, and to remain faithful to the ways of the community. If the first effect of human rituals is to make human experience supportable, its next, its concomitant effect, is to make it communal. Sacramental rituals are not only badges of a humanity that has risen above brute reaction to experience, they are also badges of community. Each community, each society, has its own 'religion', its own system of signs and the convictions which are supported by signs. So the signs which sustain a structured approach to human experience in general also allow particular groups to sustain their shared identity.

Now the church is not exempt from this. It is a community, and its sacraments are sacraments, of this type. They could be treated like any other manifestation of group religion, without respect to the truth or falsity of the faith they display. Even in that neutral perspective, it is clear that baptism and eucharist serve to identify the church and to symbolise its comprehension of life and death. It is also clear that they do not and could not stand alone.

They form part, the central part, of a wider system of signs and bearers of meaning, which necessarily includes the calling of those who minister the sacraments and apply them to the varied occasions of the community. The church is a sacramental complex to which the role of the sacramental steward – interpreting and guarding – is essential.

What distinguishes the Christian sacraments here is not their quality as communal signs, but the work of Christ by which they are informed, and which they publish. We have already frequently seen that there is a paradox here, that the order of signs should become the vehicle of the disorderly grace of a crucified God. Nevertheless, this is no more than the paradox of the church itself, that in the midst of the present age it has to live out the drastic love of the age to come.

Karl Rahner[9] sees the sacraments as the definitive acts of a church which lives in the power of Christ's eschatological victory. There is a double quality of finality which this understanding points to. First, Christ's death and resurrection bring God's work of grace to a 'victory' which is unsurpassable and indefectable. It is that categorical victory which the church is called to show forth, in dependence on the Spirit, and to give attestation to in the midst of history. Secondly the sacraments themselves are seen as decisive acts of the church, in which its official witness to the truth of God's action is fully committed. There are acts of the church – non-sacramental acts – which share in the tentative and ambiguous quality of events as much as the situations they seek to respond to. Not every pastoral action, not every pronouncement of the church can be appealed to as definitive. But the sacraments *can* be appealed to in this way. Someone can always say '*I am baptised*' (Luther) in the face of every sort of doubt. This is both the strength and the limitation of the sacramental system. The sacraments are not, themselves, except occasionally and incidentally, events in the history of the world. They are signs which relate historical events to the action of God's grace. Although they do not bring about change in the 'real' world they do hold men and women to that purpose and assurance which alone makes striving in the world possible and valuable. They enable them to be taken up and sustained in the hope that has already been fulfilled in Christ and which is moment by moment seeking fulfilment in the course of history.

That hope looks forward to a moment in which the symbolic

and the non-symbolic coincide. The sacraments do not point humankind away from social, material and embodied existence to a realm which is solitary, pure spirit, disengaged, where God is manifest apart from any medium. Rather they look to the consummation of the whole creation in glory, when God's presence within the world he has made will be fully displayed and all events, symbolic and non-symbolic, will be completed in the one supreme sacrament of a restored creation.

The church's priesthood, as a body of people called to be 'stewards of the mysteries of God', has to maintain this hope and sustain the tension between hope and present reality in its own human experience. Here too, proleptically and through much fumbling, symbolic and non-symbolic coincide. Just as in the eucharist bread and wine are placed in a new way at God's disposal in order that he can make them signs of his kingdom, so in ordination ordinary human experience is placed at God's disposal. What qualifies someone to become a Christian minister is not, either first or finally, purity or intelligence or social skill but just a capacity for being human. It is that capacity which is to be used by God to show forth his mercy and his purpose. Here again it ought not to be necessary to say that the sacramental calling of the priesthood does not detract from the sacramental status of every Christian, or every Christian's call to witness to Christ. It does not even diminish the sense in which, through baptism, every Christian is a member of every other Christian, and so is called to exercise a corporate as well as a personal moral responsibility. But the distinguishing mark of the priesthood, in the very nature of priesthood, is its visible, publicly accountable character. The priest experiences human life with all its hopes and joys, temptations and distresses, in order to stand beside other human beings and help them take hold of their own humanity in faith. His or her life is consecrated to God, not only because that is the proper goal of life, nor even because every act of self-consecration within the world serves to advance the consecration of the whole, but in order that the work of self-consecration in society might become audible and visible in a socially identifiable way. It is out of this that the pastoral responsibility of the priesthood arises – not that its members are reasonably efficient at certain 'caring' tasks, but because sensitivity to the human situation and sensitivity to the way of faith are here held together in particular people for the sake of all.

Of course this means that priests are often taken out beyond themselves, sometimes to discover gifts they could not anticipate but often only to realise their own incapacity, weakness and sin. In either condition they set themselves to be, quite deliberately, witnesses to Christ and not to themselves.

5. The Principle of Grace

There is a form of Christian rhetoric which suggests that the chasm has to open up before us if we are to perceive the goodness of God. The idea can be traced back to the Exodus tradition, when Israel is trapped between Pharaoh and the sea and Moses cries, 'Stand still, and see the salvation of the Lord' (Exod. 13.14). It is taken up in Jesus' apocalyptic promise, 'When you see these things come to pass, then look up and lift up your heads because your redemption is drawing near' (Luke 21.28). But it is St Paul who returns to this pattern with greatest frequency.

'We have had the sentence of death within ourselves, so that we should not trust in ourselves, but in God who raises the dead' (2 Cor. 1.9).

'But we have this treasure in earthen vessels, so that the exceeding greatness of the power may be from God and not from ourselves' (2 Cor. 4.7).

'As dying, and behold we live . . . as having nothing and yet possessing all things' (2 Cor. 6.9 & 10).

Faith – this seems to be the point – is a *pendent* condition; the believer hangs above the void, held by God alone. Faith comes into its own when every support except God himself is seen to have fallen away.

But that illumination, once it has shone out, can be reflected back upon other conditions in which there seems to be plenty, besides God, to rely on. Once 'the things which are seen' have been measured against the unseen grace of God, and found to be empty, faith can operate even in conditions which are visibly secure. We are not often really at the limits of human power. There are usually resources of some kind at hand. The point that has to be established is this, that while every resource can be used in faith, faith and use are distinct. Even when we find something we can do to hold ourselves above the chasm, faith works as though there were nothing we could do for ourselves. Faith recognises God alone as our helper. Once we have recognised him in that way it becomes possible to weigh up our human resources and see them as God's gift. Being saved by God, and using what lies at hand to save oneself, are no longer in conflict. The idea of synergy, of God working in and with us, is permissible and necessary to a right understanding of God, but only if the divine initiative, which God never relinquishes, is seen to be its basis. The perception is everything here. Faith looks to the unseen, and takes account of what is seen only in relation to it (2 Cor. 4.18).

The principle that we live by grace alone – 'what have you that you have not received?' (1 Cor. 4.7) – becomes not only elusive but dramatically controversial when it is applied to men's and women's moral relationship with God. God puts us right with himself by grace, and it is our faith, not our good works, which receive and answer to that grace. It seems that the best way to bring this home is to discount good works altogether, to press toward the limiting condition in which the sheer gratuitousness of God's mercy stands clear. Justification is 'apart from works', it is not 'of debt', it is the justification of the ungodly. 'God shows his love towards us in this, that while we were still sinners, Christ died for us' (Rom. 4.4 & 5; 5.8).

Yet Paul is asking for a leap of the imagination in these sayings, not for a practical testing of the idea. People are to perceive themselves as sinners, but not to behave like sinners. Few people if any are really as depraved as the limiting case requires them to be. After all Paul is speaking to Christians, and depravity like that in a Christian is unthinkable for Paul (Rom. 6.2). Justification, even if it is by faith, is a condition of righteousness, and righteousness is manifest in good works (Rom. 6.13). What Paul is objecting to is the idea that good works somehow contribute to righteousness, that grace comes not at the beginning, to establish righteousness, but at the end after works have carried us most of the way. To have faith is to recognise that, in the moral sphere as in the physical, we have nothing that we have not received. Again the recognition is everything. It is by this recognition that Christians are set free for love, that they can forget what lies behind and reach forward to what lies ahead (Phil. 3.13), that they can stop worrying whether anything stands to their credit or not.

If the ministry of the church is to be a genuine ministry of grace, it too must call for this kind of recognition, it must conform to the gospel in just this way. The earliest Christian ministry was a proclamation of the resurrection, and it seems fair to say that all subsequent ministry must be that too. It has to display God's choice of the things which are not. It has to demonstrate the Christian confidence that, through the resurrection of Jesus, God has liberated us from a hypothetical quest for grace into an affirmative confidence that grace is given.

How does the ministry of the church come to represent this recognition? One answer, which has never been positively excluded, is that it does so through spiritual gifts and miraculous events which accompany it. It is true of course that such things are often valued simply because they are effective, and most often and especially when Christians feel themselves to be socially and politically ineffective. And again such supernatural gifts can be appealed to as 'demonstrations' of the truth of faith. 'You see my works: believe my words'. There are grave dangers in all this, but beyond these somewhat crude appeals to miracle there is a more purely symbolic meaning to be found in them. Precisely because miracle is incalculable, because it cannot be built into a programme, it displays the surprising way in which God always keeps the initiative. In *this* way it reiterates the grace of the resurrection. No doubt for this reason great servants of God, especially those through whom new openings have been created for faith, are credited with miracles.

At the same time, and just because miracles and pneumatic endowments *are* incalculable, they cannot become part of the institutional character of the church. Neither the church nor the priesthood can be expected to display them on demand. That would be to turn a gift into a possession. And the point can be made as well in respect of every effect that demonstrates the power and competence of ministry. Such things are not to be despised, God wills them and bestows them, but not in such a way that we can institutionalise them.

So it turns out that the symbolic character of the Christian priesthood has this specific doctrinal character as well, that it affirms the principle of grace, even when it does so in an institutional way. The symbolic relationship with Christ is conferred, not obtained or won. It could not be otherwise. Human virtues and abilities may fit someone for the priesthood but they do not make them a priest: only the grace of a specific vocation can do that. It is in such specific vocations, conferred in fact by the Holy Spirit in response to the church's prayer at ordination, that the church finds a permanent witness to the truth that it lives by grace. Every Christian is justified, not by 'works' – that is by successes or virtues – but by grace through faith. The point is made in a symbolically more specific way, but otherwise without any difference at all, by the manner in which the Christian priesthood carries out its function. The exercise of priesthood is not justified by works, by virtues or by skills or by effectiveness, and particular ministers do not have to display these things in order to continue in ministry. On the contrary, what is required of them, and of the church which recognises its own calling in them, is that God's grace alone should be visible in them. In the limiting case, their ordination on its own, with nothing else at all, will do that, to those who perceive what ordination means.

'The unworthiness of the ministers hinders not the effect of the sacrament.'[10] This famous principle can easily be misunderstood. It does not express a preference for unworthy ministers, nor does it affirm a purely mechanical understanding of the sacraments. It does mean, though, that the Christian sacraments are sacraments of grace, that it is grace they communicate, and that grace is not made empty either by the presence or the absence of human virtue. We need the sign in order to make sense of the situation in which it appears, to expose our need of grace, and our openness to receiving it. What we cannot do is let the sign itself be obliterated, whether by the brightness of human virtue or by the darkness of human vice.

The lives of priests are sometimes seen as 'dedicated' – the fruit of a very particular consecratory intention. That is both right and wrong. All Christians are consecrated to God. The priest is not unique. But the priest's consecration is set before the church as an example of what the whole church is – not should be but is – like the active element injected into the bloodstream to make it plain where all the blood is flowing. And what is this consecratory intention? Essentially it is nothing more than an acknowledged lack of credit. Ordinands come to their ordination as approved by their fellow Christians for learning and truthfulness and godly life, and after their ordination they can expect God to add developing skills and the wisdom of experience to these human endowments. But they cannot claim credit either for what they bring or for what will come afterwards. They have to say, with St Paul, 'not I, but the grace of God in me' (1 Cor. 15.10).

6. Institution and Function

> 'This priesthood . . . is the office which ritually, inwardly and ascetically shares in the dying and rising of Christ'.[11]

Ulrich Simon's words may serve to summarise these explorations. In the Christian priesthood certain social and institutional necessities for community identity and leadership, are consecrated to the word of the cross, and so are made to serve as symbols pointing beyond themselves, sacramental witnesses to the grace of God in Christ. There are two questions which recur regularly whenever Christian ministry is discussed and it would be as well, before we finish, to ask whether this approach offers any answer to them.

The first is the question how the ordained ministry is meant to serve the unity of the church. If the church really is a social organism with its own institutions, whatever it may be beyond that, then the unity which God wills for it, and which it is bound to seek, is an institutional and visible unity. Theoretical and ultimate unity cannot be symbolised except by practical unity. Somewhere in the inevitable historical diversity of Christian response to God it has to be possible to trace some pattern of mutual accountability among Christians. The notion of social unity in the church might be taken for granted (and was up to the late middle ages) if it were not for the way the expectations it arouses have been continually baffled in practice. People appeal to an invisible church, an intangible unity, when the empirical church lets them down. Nevertheless, as successive attempts to reject the empirical demonstrate, no principled separation from the institutional church is possible without the evolution of new institutions to sustain it. The limit of our attempts to transcend the institutional is institutional schism.

And further, the institutions which result from schism always include, in some way, a ministry, a guardianship, a body of people within the whole by which the identity of the whole is signalled and guaranteed. From the second century onward, Christian bodies which broke apart did so by setting up rival ministries, and so, with some increase of sophistication, it has continued. It is natural enough then to define a state of formal schism between churches as a lack of mutual acceptability in their ministries, whether this comes about through deliberate intent, or through deliberate indifference to the question. The fact that unity breaks down in this way, by this kind of mechanism, exposes the need for a genuinely catholic ministry – one in which each minister is recognised as part of a universal as well as a local and particular priesthood. It is impossible now, events having moved as they have from so near the beginning, to attempt to recover a pristine period in the church's life when unity did not depend on ministry, when indifference to the question was innocent and not deliberate.

In fact the catholic pattern, that the local minister is a bond between the local and the whole, is normally maintained within every denominational body that practises ordination at all. The principle is generally accepted, as is the goal of social and practical unity it serves. The tragedy of denominationalism is that the unifying principle is accepted in division. The problem has become one of transcending the hold of exclusive denominational unities in the interests of a genuine ecumenical unity. A first step here might be for the ordained ministers of each and every denomination to recognise that, insofar as they have their ministry from God, they do not hold it for the sake of the *amour propre* of their own denomination. Their calling is to serve the whole. To do this humbly, without damage to one's own integrity or that of other Christians, may be an uncertain and painful experience, but at least in this way both cross and resurrection could become facts of experience within the search for Christian unity.

Nevertheless a certain sympathy is owed to those who question whether an organised ministry, and especially one with the coherence of the catholic model, can be given so prominent a place in church life. Is this not to place far too much power in the hands of fallible people?

It is here that a theological understanding of ministry is vital. The exercise of power in the church is unavoidable. The question is whether it is to be exercised simply as power – the power of personality, ability, social or bureaucratic position or whatever – or whether it is to be subject to the sacramental and symbolic function of the church. Power-structures are always symbol-structures as well. Symbolism rides upon the back of burgeoning power. We have to look up to those we follow, or suffer radical social self-doubt; symbolic power is always sought whenever the exercise of practical power is to be sustained. However, the gospel reverses the normal order. The symbol-system must define the nature and limits of practical power, not the other way round. That is not to say that if Christian leadership is exercised without ordination, it can only be perceived as the fruit of human ambition or the will to dominate. It is only to point to the way in which the symbol of ordination issues a radical challenge to reliance upon human motives. It places – admittedly in the only way it can, symbolically – the exercise of symbolic power beyond human manipulation.

Secondly, we may consider the question, often discussed, whether the relation of priests to God is functional or ontological, whether they are priests because of what they do or what they are. May it not be that both are right, in a strictly limited sense? Once it is seen that priesthood belongs to the symbolic structure of societies or social groups, then it can also be seen how both kinds of language arise and how they define each other's limits. To put it briefly, the adverb *symbolically* qualifies both the *does* and the *is* of Christian ministry.

Priesthood is functional, in that it serves a symbolic *function*. That does not conform it to other kinds of functionality – management, consultancy, education or therapy – though it may lead those who practise it into these areas. At bottom it 'works' in a different way from any of these, and makes a different kind of claim on people's attention.

But, precisely because its function is symbolic, priesthood is also ontological, it has to do with being. Priests are only perceived as priests when seen in relation to God, when their social position, personal history, interior formation are recognised as concrete symbols of God's way with humankind. Every real symbol participates in the reality it symbolises, like a poem which not only has love for its subject but the communication of love for its intention. The question about the ontological status of Christian priesthood, then, would be whether it really participates in the mystery of Christ, so as to present it to mankind.

Now the 'reality' spoken of here, in which a symbol participates, may be nothing more than the cultural reality which coheres around the symbol-system of which this symbol is part. It is the compulsions and concerted movements of feeling which sustain the unity of that culture which find their focus in the symbol. Such social symbols take their power from those who respond to them. Their energy is the energy of the people. But there can be symbols which represent mysteries that lie above and beyond culture, which cannot be analysed simply as human projections. If we are truly transcended by reality outside ourselves, the fact of our being transcended can also be symbolised. And it is axiomatic for Christian faith that, if God's transcendent grace is really manifest to us, the symbol which manifests that grace must be grounded in God, not in any human movement which seeks to construct God for itself.

And yet because the priestly symbol is itself human, and because it is located in human society, the risk that it will be distorted by cultural projection is unavoidable. It can only be met by a continual vigilance and self-purification. That is why the reality symbolised is never to be taken as God himself without further qualification. It is, rather, God in Christ, God manifest in death and resurrection, God revealed at the point where human experience meets its limit.

This last point also explains why priests' symbolic standing attaches to them personally and not just to things they do 'officially'. The distinction is valid, but the idea that the claim of God is different in the two perspectives is not. Sociologically we perceive that the claim which priesthood mediates is directed to all human life – the private life of the priest included. Theologically the point is made even more sharply. In priesthood human beings are called into conformity with Christ crucified. Neither perspective leaves the individual room into which he or she can retire away from his or her vocation. He or she is marked indelibly.

CHAPTER SEVEN

The Emergence of the Laity

that which God doth touch and own
George Herbert, *The Elixir*

1. Holy Drudgery

We are told that the word 'lay' is derived from the Greek word *laos*, and that its proper meaning is 'member of the people of God'. Such an appeal to etymology against both usage and experience shows that we are in trouble. As so often in current society, the language we use comes to us as a reflection of social relations which embarrass us. We like to think we can change the relationships by changing the language. In this case it is the negative intention of the word we want to deny – the implication that if you are not an ordained minister you are simply 'not' – you are without authority, status or power in the church. To think this is both bad theology, since it places faith and baptism behind the starting line of real Christianity, and it is bad politics, since too much depends upon the laity in the modern church, and their power is correspondingly great. Nevertheless we ought to be clear whether it is the distinction between clergy and laity in the church which is to be opposed, or a diminished understanding of the distinctive position of the laity.

Already in the New Testament the distinction is there. There are leaders and led, teachers and taught. There are those who minister in spiritual things and who can properly look for a carnal recompense. At the same time the experience of the gospel remains a common experience for all, and every Christian is held to be committed to that transformation of human life which Christ promises. It is hard to believe that this sense of common enterprise has been sustained throughout all the ages of the Church, even if we have to admit to caution in judging what this might have meant in the multitude of social situations the church has had to live with. It seems that, whatever may have been gained theologically and effectively by the rise of an institutional ministry, there has been a corresponding loss to those who are not included in it. The sense of loss is there, in the church as it is today. We do not have to hark back to old scandals, to draw this out. It is better that we shouldn't, since the sense of scandal is often our projection on to a situation we do not understand. We have only to look at the way many of the laity now see themselves as the clients of the clergy, without competence or scope for ministry of their own. Contemporary theology condemns that, and no reference to a past golden age is needed to help it do so.

Historical reference has another purpose – to help us see how we arrived at our present position, and to recognise the matrix of thought and sentiment within which our current judgements take their place. And for that purpose the most valuable period to study is the Reformation, for it is the unfinished business of the Reformation which still perplexes the church today. It is in the Reformation period that lay people as we know them today first appear, as part of a cultural landscape we can still recognise as our own, however much the machines have worked over it since. And the answers to the lay predicament first canvassed at that time are still, largely, those that we try to apply.

The Elixir

Teach me, my God and King,
In all things Thee to see,
And what I do in any thing
To do it as for Thee.

Not rudely, as a beast,
To runne into an action;
But still to make Thee prepossest,
And give it his perfection.

A man that looks on glasse,
On it may stay his eye;
Or if he pleaseth, through it passe,
And then the heav'n espie.

All may of Thee partake:
Nothing can be so mean
Which with his tincture, 'for Thy sake,'
Will not grow bright and clean.

A servant with this clause
Makes drudgery divine;
Who sweeps a room as for Thy laws
Makes that and th' action fine.

This is the famous stone
That turneth all to gold;
For that which God doth touch and own
Cannot for lesse be told.

This poem by George Herbert can be read as a late-reformation document whose interpretation will shed light, not merely on the poet's mind, or on the subject matter it discusses, but on a considerable shift of perception which came about during the reformation era. John Wesley turned it into a hymn by leaving out the second verse, and in that form it says something people still want to say to God. Even without the second verse an air of obscurity remains, but the main route through is well marked – the almost prosaic first verse which fixes the theme, and then the motto 'for thy sake' and then the servant with her sweeping brush who reminds us so much of ourselves. Here is something which is both straightforward and good. The humblest action can be done for God's sake, and God is to be served in all we do. Come on – the hymn seems to say – what are you waiting for?

Yet waiting appears to be part of Herbert's intention. Even without the unsingable second verse, the hymn invites reflection, and commits us *to* reflection. When Herberts prays, 'Teach me', we can take it that he means it. The words are neither redundant nor a disguise for, 'Let me teach *you*, dear reader!' The image of the beast that runs rudely into action is really essential to the argument; it is not in rude haste but in stillness – as standing *still* before God – that we make him *prepossest* of ourselves and our deeds. We do not, after all, see God in all things by plain observation. We do need to be taught, trained and above all enlightened if base metal is to be transmuted into gold in our everyday experience. Herbert is not announcing a platitude; he is seeking a revelation.

But what, we may say, about divine drudgery? That at least is a Christian commonplace. Well, perhaps so, and if so it might stand as an answer to our problem about the calling of lay Christians. If even drudgery can be divine then any honest work, any socially useful task, is worthy of God as well. That is what we are affirming when we sing these words, and we assume that Herbert takes it for granted too.

But again, is Herbert as a late-reformation Christian as certain in this matter as we are? or as John Keble seemed to be?

> We need not bid, for cloistered cell,
> Our neighbour and our work farewell . . .
>
> The trivial round, the common task,
> Would furnish all we ought to ask, – . . .

Holy drudgery is nothing new in Christian experience, but it has not always had the same character. Four centuries back from Herbert we find St Francis and his followers abandoning comfort and privilege to become poor menials in the service of others, but in a style quite different from Herbert's servant. Francis' life stands out as a fairly healthy example of a style of piety that sometimes took much more extravagant and self-lacerating forms – a piety rooted in fascination for the suffering and humiliated Christ. The elixir here is not so much 'for thy sake' as 'in thine image', whether one is conformed to that image oneself by voluntary poverty and self-humiliation or one recognises it in those one serves – themselves, humble, poor and suffering. It is the voluntary quality of these actions, the deliberate going beyond social necessity, which makes them worthy of God in mediaeval piety. The absence of any such quality in Herbert is noteworthy. He is not offering to do the works of a housemaid himself, nor is his housemaid really a rich laywoman looking for a special way of showing her devotion. She is simply a housemaid, doing what she is bound to do.

And yet, in a curious reversal of this contrast we can also see Herbert's piety as essentially voluntaristic, and mediaeval piety as a simple acknowledgement of what is given. The servant in Herbert's poem sweeps because she must, but she has to choose to find sanctity in it, she has to bring the elixir to it by an inward disposition of her own. By contrast, Francis finding Christ in the poor and in lepers was as firmly assured of his objective presence there as he was in respect of the blessed sacrament. His holy drudgery was as much a form of sacral worship as a Corpus Christi procession, or a pilgrimage to the shrine of a saint.

A pilgrimage shrine is objectively holy. That is why it is visited. People do not sanctify it by their devotion. They offer devotion because holiness has already discovered itself in that place. And even to speak of devotion may be treacherous if we understand it in our own post-reformation terms. Pilgrimage devotion – Chaucer will give sufficient witness – was quite consistent with a good deal of seeming irreverence, and with a lack of quiet recollection, for the purpose of the pilgrimage was not essentially to achieve that or any other inward state but to go, to touch, to see, to inhabit the place which possessed this objective holiness.

Now it is this sense that holiness is simply there, in things, in people, in words, in symbols and ceremonies, which gave lay devotion in the middle ages its special character. Lay Christians were made aware that they belonged, to God, to the church and to the saints, by the stake they had in the palpable givenness of the sacral system. The mass, the priesthood, church buildings, and all the holy objects circulating around them, while in one sense set apart from the laity, in another way made the sacred fully available to them. Human life was sanctified by contact with holy people, holy actions, holy things. It was not that lay people could not share in holiness, nor that their holiness was merely passive, but that it could not be achieved except by resort to the church's cultus, to the system of rite and symbol that confronted society as simply there. That is why trades and occupations which, to us, are worthy of respect in themselves, were organised in the mediaeval period through guilds which were as much sacral brotherhoods as professional associations. It was through their patron saints, their chapels and chaplains, their special part in communal religious festivals, that the work of the guild's members was sanctified. It was not considered holy because it was human work, because God had ordained it or provided for it in the created order; it had to be made holy by contact with those things which were especially holy already, in a distinct and (to us) quite non-utilitarian way.

So when we find a new concern springing up, in Francis and the movements that followed him, for simplicity, poverty and humility, we have to see that these qualities are being treated as repositories of objective holiness, and not merely as virtues that a seeker after holiness would naturally display. No doubt squalor, ignorance, want and pain were commonplace in mediaeval society, but they were not regarded as holy in their commonplaceness. It was because Christ had placed himself within them that they were holy, and so held out a special attraction to those who could otherwise have gone free of them. We see this in the way poverty, simplicity and sometimes voluntary pain are made central to the rules of orders and brotherhoods which lay people increasingly joined. It was as though, like the dignified crafts, poverty had been given its own guild. It was not the condition of humiliation in society as such, but a proficient and sacrally recognised humiliation, which gave lay people an assurance of belonging to a world really made over to God.

2. Luther and the Laity

In his Greater Catechism, on the commandment, 'You shall honour your father and your mother,' Martin Luther[1] had written this.

> 'What a child owes to father and mother, the entire household owes them likewise. Therefore man-servants and maid-servants should take care not only to obey their masters and mistresses, but also to respect them as their own parents and do everything that they know is expected of them, not from compulsion and reluctantly but gladly and cheerfully; and they should do it for the reason just mentioned, that it is God's commandment and more pleasing to him than all other works. They ought even to be willing to pay for the privilege of service and be glad to acquire masters and mistresses in order to have such joyful consciences and know how to do truly golden works. These works in the past have been neglected and despised; instead everybody ran in the devil's name into monasteries, on pilgrimages and after indulgences, to their own hurt and with a bad conscience.'
>
> 'If this truth could be impressed upon the poor people, a servant girl would dance for joy in praise and thank God . . . Is it not a wonderful thing to be able to boast to oneself. "If I do my daily housework faithfully, that is better than the holiness and austere life of the monks"?'

Unlike Herbert, who still asks to be taught, Luther speaks here with the exuberance of one who knows. It does not cross his mind that someone might seriously debate whether to pay for the privilege of service. There is no need. Works worth searching out do not in fact have to be sought, in the way works of piety have to be sought. The order of society provides them – the very order of nature.

Luther's two catechisms, his most deliberate and comprehensive address to the laity, read strangely to those who know him only by reputation. There is nothing here of justification by faith, nothing of the universal priesthood of the church. Instead he begins and for a good while goes on with the word of God in the Ten Commandments. It is true that this serves a theological strategy, since he sees the Commandments as an impossible target, and consequently a revelation of God's wrath and an exposure of our need of grace. Yet, equally theologically, he sees them as a social programme and a clear declaration of the way God intends to sanctify human life. Not in the monastery but in society as it is, God calls us to a holy blessedness.

For Luther, the family is the root of all social existence under God. Parents are God's representatives to their children, marriage is a state, 'blessed above all others', and in neither case does this divinely given quality derive from some special consecration that has to be obtained. The natural, here, does not have to be made holy; it is holy because it is natural, because God's creative providence works through it. People, then, are not to find their work for God through special 'holy' vocations which they have to support with unusual labours, but rather through social institutions that God has provided for all and protected by commandments addressed to all.

And what the family is, so society is – a system of mutual relationships grounded in faithfulness, a system of hierarchies in which rulers command and provide, subjects honour and obey. Luther stresses obedience again and again, there is no morality without it, but for him human obedience is always conditioned by an awareness of God as the one alone who has the right to command majestically. In human society obedience is owed to those who are themselves charged with the onerous duty of ruling, that is, of putting God's providential purpose into effect. 'Through civil rulers, as through our own parents, God gives us food, house and home, protection and security. Therefore, since they bear the name and title which all honour as their chief glory, it is our duty to honour and magnify them as the most precious treasure and jewel upon earth'.[2]

So when people carry out the work that belongs to their station in society, they do more than obey the command of God, they cooperate with him in the ordering of the world and become the means through which he personally acts. 'What is meant by daily bread?' Luther asks, and provides the answer, 'Everything required to satisfy our bodily needs, such as food and clothing, house and home, fields and flocks, money and property; a pious spouse and good children, trustworthy servants, godly and faithful rulers, good government; seasonable weather, peace and health, order and honour; true friends, faithful neighbours and the like.' This is God's provision, this is what he teaches us to expect from him, but it is also for the most part a social provision and it is from men and women in society that we are to expect it. The providence of God really works through the actions of humankind, provided men and women act in truth and goodness.[3]

Nothing could show more clearly how Luther conceives the vocation of the laity. If you want to draw near to God, to know that he acknowledges you and unites himself with you, you need not budge from where you are already. It is in the place each of us occupies simply as a human being that we are to find God.

This natural way, however, is no broad path. It is clearly menaced from both sides. On the one hand Luther fears that the autonomy he recognises will spill over into licence. 'They live as if they were pigs and irrational beasts, and now that the Gospel has been restored they have mastered the fine art of abusing liberty'. On the other hand, as his frequent sideswipes at the Carthusians and other monks show, he is afraid that the old sacral heteronomy will return, that people will still seek recognition from God in unusual devotions and ecclesiastical works. Temptation hides itself within the promise of liberty but also within the call to piety. Behind his insistence on the common and everyday was his discovery that God's promise of mercy could be met there without any disturbance of its natural order. All that was required was trust in his word and a proper understanding of baptism. For Luther all Christian vocation is comprehended in baptism; nothing needs to be added to it.[4] It claims and sanctifies the whole of life. The way to serve God is to let the death and resurrection of Christ, which it figures, work in us day by day whatever circumstances we find ourselves in. Baptism is not a past event, which we have to improve upon by additional works of our own. It is an ever present work of God upon us, to which we can in every moment respond.

And it is upon baptism that Luther builds his understanding of the relationship between clergy and laity, and his claim that the laity, just as much as the clergy, are priests.

Luther is never easy to systematise, and here especially he resists both careful systematisation and easy sloganising – though not averse to composing slogans himself when politics require. Here the point can be made both negatively and positively. Negatively, 'In Christ there is neither lay nor cleric, nor status of this nor that order. Such things do not make a believer if present, nor an infidel if absent.'[5] Here we are invited to take an ultimate perspective, not by abolishing distinctions between clergy and laity, but recognising that they are transcended in our direct meeting with God. Before God[6] a Christian is simply a Christian, a baptised believer, a forgiven sinner, whatever he or she may be called in human society. On the other hand, in his fiercely political and somewhat opportunist appeal to the Christian Nobility, Luther insists that, even as laymen they are of the spiritual elect, all of them 'priests, bishops and popes', and therefore competent to undertake the reform and liberation of the church.[7] Here implicitly is the doctrine that commentators will extract laboriously from Luther's writings, that lay Christians have a real priesthood which they exercise by fulfilling their secular calling in a godly way. It is not, of course, by some appeal to lay democracy but because God has made them rulers that Luther regards the nobility as the appropriate people to make provision for the church. The idea that baptism and faith as such should qualify someone for public function in the church is one that Luther explicitly rejects.[8]

At this point we have to wrestle with the paradoxical dualism in Luther's theology. It seems that in the temporal order God has set forth the nature of our callings and offices with great clarity, and we can confidently affirm that what we do represents his will and serves his action. In the spiritual sphere this is not so. The full realisation of our spiritual status is held back from us. God reigns in both the temporal and spiritual kingdoms, but he has not yet subjected the one to the other, and so Christians have to wait for their inheritance in hope, struggling with the contradictions of the present order.

It is not surprising then that people feel that Luther wants to affirm the priesthood of all the baptised[9] and yet at the same time refuses to give this principle any systematic practical expression. At the most it comes down to a number of explanations about the ordained ministry – not its abolition, but an interpretation of its status and purpose. It is better not called a priesthood, though in some of his polemical works Luther does call it a priesthood and regards it as a paradigm, on the bodily level, of what all Christians are called to be spiritually. It is not a sacrificing priesthood, but a ministry of the word and of pastoral care. It is not permanent in character, even if it is held as a life-long office. When all this is said, the 'called and consecrated ministry' remains, and lay people are not to intrude upon it. That is not seemly, nor is it proper. What belongs to all cannot be exercised by one except by authority.[10]

In all this Luther seems to exclude the layman from the ecclesiastical sphere – unless he is a prince – quite as firmly as anyone in the mediaeval period. The idea that the priesthood of lay people is worked out in their secular calling – or more strictly that the spiritual priesthood of every Christian is worked out in his or her social calling – could be put down as no more than a compensating device. Lay priesthood in the traditional sense of priesthood comes no nearer in Luther than in Aquinas. Nevertheless, we should allow that this was Luther's position, and that he had good theological reasons for taking it.

The first was that the priesthood of the church is a spiritual, and therefore eschatological reality. It cannot be realised in the present age. The 'bodily' action of the ordained minister certainly does not realise it. At best it points visibly and socially to an invisible and personal reality to which all have equal access. Luther could incorporate the laity into this bodily priesthood only at the cost of his social teaching, which was as we have seen thoroughly affirmative of the present order yet thoroughly eschatological.

But secondly, for Luther, the ecclesiastical is the sphere of false piety, of self-justifying works, of the graceless refusal to submit to God either in faith or in obedience. Luther had no desire to perpetuate sacralism, even in an evangelical form. If God had given people autonomy in temporal matters, they must not surrender it to the church. If holiness was to be found through worldly obedience, it must be sought in that way, and that way only.

Luther's attitude to human temporal autonomy shows us both what he took from the humanism of his time and what he rejected. Whether either acceptance or rejection was wholly deliberate, and deliberately stated, is not the issue here. We are looking at Luther rather as a social weathercock, a medium through which diffuse social attitudes get expressed, sometimes against his own will and judgement. Luther seems to have had a peculiar sensitivity in these matters, an ability to articulate what others were only feeling. That is why, in the short term, he had more allies than, in the long term, he wanted to acknowledge – why the anti-clericals, the German nationalists, the humanistic scholars and lawyers, the middle-class capitalists and the down-trodden peasants all heard him saying things they wanted to hear, and were prepared to let him run for a time. No doubt the existence of these allies tipped the balance between success and failure in his life's work, but they were not all equally important to him, and some had obviously mistaken his meaning. But the question of humanism is central.

3. Constructive Revolution

Humanism takes many forms,[11] but all raise the question of authority and decide that, in some matters at least, humanity alone can be the judge. In this respect every kind of humanism challenged the mediaeval ideal – never perhaps realised in fact – that all knowledge and all rule should be comprehended in one divinely given system. Emperors and Popes had fought one another, throughout the middle ages, temporal and spiritual were properly distinguished, but distinguished as parts of a whole, with the expectation that God could be seen to arbitrate between them in some clear and palpable way. Humanism challenges that, not necessarily by challenging God himself, nor even by challenging the Church's title to speak of divine things, but by shifting theology as the science of divine things to a position *among* the other sciences and not over them. There was indeed a paganising humanism around in Luther's time, though more so in Italy than Germany, which set human powers at the centre of the world and made us creators of our own values and destiny. Machiavelli – both in his ideas and in his reputation – can stand for that. But a more subtle relation with tradition was represented by scientific humanism, by the emergence of scholarly disciplines that took new confidence in enquiry, experience, and reason to answer questions. And even more subtle, for here there was long continuity as well as new insight, was Christian humanism, such as shaped the life of Erasmus and gave Calvin his education. Here the rational and scientific spirit was not opposed to faith, nor indifferent to it, but (at least in principle) given over to its service. Christian humanists used their humanist confidence to make fresh appeals to scripture and the fathers, and to criticise the contemporary church in the light of what they found. What all these have in common is a sense that human ideas and human actions can no longer be ordered in one hierarchical scheme, with all truth and value being handed down from the top. Every answer to every question now invites another question – Who says so? – and another – How do they know? And there is no agreement that every chain of enquiry will eventually lead back to the same source – certainly not to a source within the church.

That means, in turn, that as thinker and as agent, a person is autonomous in relation to the church, even (though the conditions may be hard to specify) in strictly ecclesiastical matters.

It is not hard to see, then, why for a time Luther and the humanists were perceived as allies in their challenge to an older perception of ecclesiastical authority. For Luther, more through instinct than by persuasion, also acknowledged that people are autonomous in temporal things. There really are, for him, arts and disciplines that have their own rationality and owe nothing to divine revelation. A Turk will rule a country quite as well as a Christian, provided only that both are guided by reason.[12] The church has a strictly circumscribed role in human affairs, and most human life is lived outside its direct authority. But, and this is Luther's distinctive point, it is not lived outside God's authority. Luther had no desire to bring the world's concerns back under the shelter of the church, but then, as he understood it, to attempt such a thing would be to fall from faith, not to express it. God had made temporal society autonomous in relation to the church. The Christian must serve God within it on its own terms, but – that was the point – by serving society on its own terms he or she would also be obediently serving God.

Luther lived at a time when a new lay culture, *un esprit laic*, was coming into existence, and his achievement here was to have perceived that God had no essential quarrel with that culture, nor with its citizens. They are still his servants – better servants now, since at last they have recognised where true service lies, not in the accumulation of ecclesiastical credit but in citizenship, in neighbourliness, in daily work and family life. Luther's lay people are recognisably modern in this respect, and as a pastoral theologian he still speaks to the modern world. He followed sound instincts and set things off in the right direction.

Any attempt to re-establish a sacral culture in the face of human autonomy, as attempted by the counter-reformation and its successors, could only be a delaying tactic, and one that would impose insupportable strains on human integrity. On this point Luther was right. The temporal order did not require more priests in the sanctuary than it had already, not though all men and women in their spiritual standing were priests to God. The work of God was to be done outside the sanctuary, in the world.

But if we ask him what that work is, and how we are to do it, he leaves us disappointed. He has only one word for us – obey – and it is not enough. Luther's social conservatism protected him from internal challenge at this point. Perhaps he found the existential insecurity of trusting God in the face of contradiction quite enough. He would not turn society into the adventure playground of faith as well. In Luther's scheme God shapes and guides the lives of individuals through the ordering of society, but the ordering of society is taken as given. The question is never asked, what of change in society? – how is that to be guided and shaped?

Herbert's doctrine on this point must seem to be more modern still than Luther's, for Herbert was consciously perplexed by the social changes going on around him.[13] Luther's servant girl knows quite simply that her works are golden. Herbert's has to pray for a right perception.

Like his contemporary, Columbus, Luther had come to the edge of a new world and claimed it, before any exploration, for his King. The society of the future would be secular, but that did not mean it would have to be godless. The new found dignity of man was to be matched by a recovered dignity among the Christian laity, who would occupy this new found land and serve God there. Secularity was to be embraced and not opposed in the name of God. Luther was following a consistent strategy here. His main object was to set Christians free from alienating piety. His own experience had shown him the need, the evident corruption of the church enabled him to share his concern with others, and the emergence of a secular world gave him a territory in which the experiment of living a godly life outside the sanctuary could be pursued.

It is more questionable whether he achieved moral consistency in the way he handled this. Even if the doctrine of the two kingdoms is not to be blamed for the emergence of Hitler, Christians are bound to be uneasy about a system of thought that makes such a sharp and unalterable distinction between Christian and public virtue, which tells the hangman to meet those he executes with godly love and secular severity at one and the same time.[14] Can the conscience be so easily stilled – by allowing God and the delay of his kingdom to take all the blame?

Not all the reformers thought so. Calvin did not, and it is to Calvin rather than to Luther that we look first for a more constructive approach to the idea of secular action in the service of God.[15] Calvin was less ready to regard society simply as God's department of restraining law, less prepared to treat the redemption of human kind purely in terms of hope and endurance. In his view a church that could achieve godly discipline within itself would also achieve substantial changes in the lives of its members, and where that church's members and society's members were the same, the presence of the church in society could have some redemptive effect even on social affairs. This would not mean reviving the attempt to regulate society through the church, as some mediaeval theories implied and as some of Calvin's successors seem to have attempted. It means only that Christians could be expected to behave like Christians in their secular callings as well as in church, to avoid evil and to seek to do good, and that the church might well be able to offer them support and advice as to ways, means and occasions for appropriate action.

At the level of church polity this will work well only if the common membership of church and society is assumed, but the principle at stake is independent of these circumstances. Whereas Luther believed that unaugmented reason could guarantee good government, the Calvinist tradition allows that perceptions that are peculiarly Christian can enter into the practice of politics. The effect of this is that for a strict Lutheran a political issue cannot become a question of faith, though it can of course be a question of truth. For those whose reformation instincts go back to Calvin (even when they do not know it) there remains always the question whether the gospel itself does not have a bearing on political and social behaviour.

The two servant girls – Luther's and Herbert's – illustrate this difference, not at the level of theory but existentially. Luther's girl knows where she is, and she rejoices accordingly. Herbert's awkward second verse shows the awkwardness of his perception. Actions have to be weighed before being performed. God must be 'prepossest' – given first claim – and that cannot be taken for granted without reflection. Really, when compared with Luther's, Herbert's idea of the union of Christian faith with secular action is more interesting, because potentially quite subversive. There is no guarantee that normal arrangements will be left to stand as they are, that nothing will be challenged, that the Christian conscience may not propose a reform of manners or even of society. It has been suggested that when, in his fifth verse, Herbert speaks of 'that which God doth touch and own' he means touch with his touchstone – put to the test. God may be in all things, but to perceive him and act on his behalf requires a certain kind of vision, an appetite for truth.

CHAPTER EIGHT

Secularisation and the Church's Priesthood

. . . it is easy to miss Him
at the turn of a civilisation.
David Jones, *A, a, a, Domine Deus.*

1. The Nature of the Change

We have seen that from earliest times societies have developed priesthoods in order to articulate the relationship between themselves and the sacred. Christians have developed this idea to show how, through Christ and the Holy Spirit, the whole of human existence is laid open to God, is enabled to realise his saving presence, and is consecrated to him. More than that, because human existence is inseparable from the world of which it is part, this consecratory priesthood is meant to be effective for all creation. This basic idea has developed in two distinct and seemingly contradictory directions.

On the one hand it is frankly recognised that the service of God has to take an institutional form if it is really to affect society and the world. Those to whom God has entrusted the good news of his love must allow themselves to become the focus of social expectations, the turbulent centre of social affections. The church has to provide, through its own ministry, a sacral priesthood for all people. It must go beyond recognising its own identity in certain institutional signs, as any self-aware group would do: it has to let those signs become part of the total social system. Only so can the claim of God in every area of human concern be demonstrated. Only so can every human sensibility be challenged to recognise the ways in which God lays claim to its service and pledges his grace. This is the rationale for the church's ministerial priesthood.

The other line of development starts from the conviction that God has given us, through Christ, a liberty in relation to himself that transcends all institutions. We have to recognise that if God has really brought us near to himself then we have been defeated, radically and once and for all, in our attempts to fashion for ourselves a pattern of being with God. However subtle our formulae, however transparent our institutions, the knowledge of God exceeds our capacity to articulate it. Along this line of argument, priesthood is not a matter of set forms and predictable rites. It is rather a claim and a promise addressed to all human beings, a summons to them to recognise the work of the Creator through the way they live in his creation. And even if the whole human race has been exposed as a failure in the face of this claim, and the claim itself nullified since no one can respond to it, still the Church of Christ has to maintain it, since in Christ mankind has been recalled to it and given the grace to realise it afresh. On this basis we speak of the universal priesthood of the church, and the priesthood of all humankind.

If these two perceptions are to be held together, then the first form of priesthood must see itself as ancillary to the second. It has to state the unstateable in ordinary human language. The institution must exist, not as a restraint upon the priesthood which is restored to all humankind in Christ, but as the means by which that priesthood is signified and sustained. If the church allows some of its members to become sacral priests in society it is not so that those members should become a separate and privileged tribe, but so that the privilege of the gospel should be more readily and unaggressively shared with everyone.

That twofold perception of the Church's priesthood was already at work in the first century when faith in Christ necessarily, though not without risk, suffered formulation in credal statements and patterns of confession. The same perception was there in the fourth century when the Church accepted worldliness as its vocation for the sake of the world which God had redeemed. It was there in the sixteenth century, when the rediscovery of Christian antistructure led, not to a destructuring but to a restructuring of priestly and institutional forms.

At that latter stage, as we have seen, the issue came to centre on the status of lay Christians. It would be intolerable – so it was perceived – if their share in the priestly calling of the church, and hence in Christian freedom before God, were any longer to be denied. And yet the new affirmations could not escape the old potential contradiction. Is the priesthood in which the laity share something that only the inner life of the Church can demonstrate?

Or is it, as Luther and Calvin affirmed, an inspiration to a new Christian engagement with the secular life of mankind? These are not questions which a church can answer for itself. The church does not define for itself where the boundaries of its own internal affairs run. That is done through its interaction with society, and society contributes to the definition.[1] And the church cannot specify exactly what kind of people its lay members are to be, and how they are to share in its priesthood, since various social situations open up new possibilities to the church's members, and impose various kinds of constraint upon them. Luther's notions about the Christian calling of masters and servants were becoming out of date even while he formulated them. If the church is to be constructively engaged with society as a whole it has to take account of the way society is evolving, and here we draw near to the crisis of modern church life, for since the sixteenth century, western society has been evolving in ways which do not encourage such constructive engagement.

The word 'secularisation' has not proved easy to define[2] but, for all that, has not been easy to avoid, either, in recent pastoral theology. It is, it seems, the one word we can use with mutual confidence when we want to say that the pastoral situation has changed since – let us say – the industrial revolution. Even if the precise nature of the change is elusive it is clear that many activities go on that were once naturally referred to God and no longer are. There was a time when religious symbolism was felt to be relevant to family life, education, citizenship and politics, and to healing the sick and relieving the poor. Now these things go on without any frequent religious reference, and sometimes none at all. At the same time, sociologists (whose particular field this is) disagree among themselves as to what really constitutes secularisation, and are much less inclined than some theologians to label the whole modern world secular without further discussion. Much theological writing of the last generation started off from the assertion that no one really counted as modern unless he or she were – in some sense of the term – an atheist. Or, it might be, faith in God could continue in some form, but traditional expressions would no longer carry it. In any case, and however we interpreted the word, the genuinely modern world was secular, and what was not secular was anachronistic. Time, as it always does, would take care of the anachronisms. Serious discussion had to assume a secular basis.

Any substance in this hypothesis was given to it by the effect of technology upon human life. Technology does at least two things to human culture. It makes life more predictable, and it forces us to organise ourselves in ways which correspond with that predictability.[3] It was the first of these effects that seemed to give the secularist view intellectual weight. If we are no longer at the mercy of capricious powers, if we can look after ourselves, then we do not need the reassurances that religion brings, and traditional religious forms have no further practical meaning. If faith is to continue into this new, secular world, it will have to take forms which are consistent with the secular understanding of humanity and nature.

This thesis was always vulnerable to a more subtle hypothesis, or to a more accurate description of the situation. It began to appear, when people actually looked, that religion was really more persistent in the modern world than had been allowed. Certainly it might take on new forms, as evidenced by Western interest in Eastern religion, or by the surge of charismatic activity in the traditional churches. It might seem that while for much of a person's life the thesis was true – religion made no practical difference – yet at one or two points it could matter intensely. The clergy were frequently baffled by parents who never came near church at other times but insisted tenaciously on having their babies baptised. Whether this was labelled superstition, folk religion, or mere convention, it was not consistent with the thesis of inexorable and total secularisation. In a secular world superstition ought to disappear before rational religion does, not after it. Truly autonomous man has no need to make propitiatory gestures to Lady Luck. And if, on the other hand, much religion in the modern world tends toward an interest in the exotic and the novel, that is something that needs to be included in the explanatory thesis and not dismissed by it.

A more durable thesis than that of mandatory secularity for modern people, and of more superficial plausibility, is that the world has reverted to a form of pre-Christian paganism, leaving the church free to recover its pristine, first-century faith. Seen in this way the problems of modern Christians over against society can be interpreted as reversions to New Testament types. Christians are once again on their own in a hostile, unbelieving world, except so far as a self-conscious, deliberately fostered Christian fellowship sustains them. Individual conversion becomes the distinguishing mark of real Christian faith. The world – society outside the church – is defined negatively. Its natural bent is to resist conversion. The religion which persists in society, however much it may make claims upon the Church and draw upon Christian tradition, can be explained simply as the last form of that paganism which popular Christianity has always tried to exploit. But we know better now than to try to be popular.

Morally and factually this position is false. Its air of self-congratulation is not deserved, its confusion between failure to communicate and victory for truth is merely desperate, and its reading of modern society is not justified. The truth is that the modern church is in no way a replication of the first century church nor could it be. Its historical situation is different, and so are the social functions it most successfully serves. If modern Christians find resonances between the New Testament and their own experience it could be because prejudices fostered in our own time are often brought to the reading of the scriptures. We find our own situation in the New Testament because we are determined to do so, not because it is really there. A sense of moral and emotional *déjà vu* obscures the factual differences between that age and our own.

We need to stand somewhere else and look afresh. If it is not possible, without self-deception, to attach one diagnostic label to the whole of modern culture, that may be because modern culture is not a unity. There is in it no single picture of the world and our place within it which commands general assent. On the other hand there are perspectives on human experience, limited in their application, restricted to this or that matter only, which do command such assent. There are assumptions about technological activity which are shared by all who engage in it, and the same is true of pure science, of commerce and industry, of government, of warfare, of art and recreation. Each of these pursuits can claim to constitute a 'world' in itself. True, the different worlds interact, and people have roles to play in several of them or in all, but they are not reducible to a single world. Modern culture is differentiated, a nexus of cultures without centre or circumference. Different spheres of activity within it carry different systems of value, different principles of action, different canons of truth or propriety.

The scholars of the Renaissance led the way in this when they developed their autonomous disciplines. A view of learning in which it could be claimed that all knowledge was ordered, not too remotely, about a single centre – a centre which could only be the knowledge of God – gave way to one in which each discipline was found interesting in itself. New scientific methods were worked out, each conformable to its own subject matter and not to some universal definition of true science. Experience was laid open to fresh analysis, authority exposed to questioning. The assumed unity of knowledge was dissolved. In particular a distinction could be made between natural knowledge and theology, between humanity as agent in the world and as worshipper. This did not mean that people of affairs ceased to be believers, but it did mean (as we have seen) that people could go about their business without continual reference to the symbols of their faith.

This desacralisation of culture developed into full-blown secularisation as the new sciences gave rise to new technologies. Differentiated science allows people to think in several independent modes. Technology subjects them to independent systems of activity.[4] We may assume that the principal effect of technology in human life is the increased control it gives us over our condition, but in the long run technology's control over us is more important. To use technology we have to submit to it. We have to re-order our world on a scale that makes it economically possible to use it, and in the process, paradoxically, human endeavour falls apart in new and massive divisions of labour. We end up, not with one technology but many, serving the interests of different activities – economic, bureaucratic, propagandist – each provided with its own system, its own axioms, its own methods and its own goals.

The world before the technological revolution can be likened to an olympic boat crew, subject in each of its members (that is, its disciplines) to a single controlling discipline, motivated by a single seriousness of purpose, aiming at perfect coordination. Our modern world, by comparison, is like the third eight of a small college. Its members (again, its disciplines) have no common ambition, they undertake no common commitment, they rub along together for mutual convenience without even the need to define that convenience. Each is satisfied in his own way if the venture continues somehow. Physically they may all be in the same boat, but according to purpose and motive they are not all going the same way.

So it is in our own modern differentiated culture. Assuming, as an ideal construction, a time in the past when all organised activities took place within an overarching framework, we can say that society is perceptibly moving further and further away from such a state. The great organised sectors of life do not now so much serve a single end as serve one another as each pursues its own end. Trade interacts with production at one point, the legal profession at another. Private individuals buy for personal sustenance and gratification, perhaps at the behest of advertisers and perhaps in keeping with their own eccentric tastes. Governments regulate these things in order to tax them, and in the interest of ideologies that are neither coherent nor uncontested. No activity needs to justify itself in terms of ultimate values: its social viability is justification enough. No total framework of interpretation is needed: each kind of activity can explain itself to itself in its own way. And none needs God to propose theories or to set goals. Each can go ahead with a rationality of its own, without any reference to religion.

In this sense the modern public world is godless – not pagan but godless – and faith, when it tries to engage with the public world, faces a massive indifference. But in no way can this situation be likened to that of Christians in the ancient world, when it was the Christians and not the pagans who seemed to their neighbours to be atheists. Nor does the split between godlessness and faith run between groups in society – the church against the rest. It runs through the heart of each person, for there is no one who does not share somehow in the public world, and so in its godlessness. Christian and non-Christian alike have to cope with this split within themselves – the fact that ultimate commitment calls for a personal faith to which the great public processes are indifferent.

Alongside the public world lies the private world – something completely new in human experience, though we may be surprised to recognise it as such. Unified culture leaves no space for privacy as we know it. Only as culture breaks apart into fragments, do gaps appear within which private activity can go on unsupervised, unregulated, apparently nobody's business.[5] It is when work begins to be measured out in parts of the day and week that leisure emerges, defined as the time in which people can do what they want and are not answerable to anyone else. It is here that the concept of personal autonomy is fostered. Leisure and liberty run together.

It may be, though, that leisure, such as it is, fosters the illusion of a liberty which neither it, nor the public world, really provides. Have we really so great a field of choice? Ralf Dahrendorf in his Reith Lectures spoke of 'overdetermined work and underdetermined leisure'.[6] As workers today, people have little scope to plan their own course in the public world. They must respond to the demands of the market, conform to the technology they serve. The sense of initiative atrophies, and even outside their public time, after work and after retirement, little presents itself worthy of a fully human commitment. Thomas Luckmann speaks of the triviality of private choices.[7] The momentous events, that shape history and make for justice or injustice, happen in the public sphere, precisely where the initiative of the individual counts for little. In the private sphere the same individual is faced with a bewildering range of possibilities, all equally acceptable to society, all as likely as not to amuse or instruct him, but all equally insignificant upon the public stage. Even those personal acts which appear to have an impact upon public affairs, like voting in an election, or selecting one particular product in preference to another, only lose significance again when they are seen as tiny contributions to a statistical aggregate whose behaviour may well be predictable, and even, though one hardly knows by whom, manipulable.

Now it is within this area of uncertain significance, the realm of private motivation, that modern religion is placed. Peter Berger cites the American phrase, one's 'religious preference'.[8] Going to this or that church is like ordering a drink in a bar, a matter of consumer choice. In England, religious disputes are impolite because religion is a private matter. Politicians tell the church to keep out of politics, appealing to ancient wisdom as they conceive it against novel tendencies to politicise the gospel. In a certain public context it becomes inconceivable that religious convictions could make any real difference to what happens.

We may be glad that modern culture is not enclosed within a single, religiously sustained, interpretative framework – tyrannous and idolatrous at the same time. Nevertheless the cost of modern existential freedom is very high – the loss of the sense of destiny, the severance of the links between personal freedom and publicly recognised responsibility. Berger and his colleagues speak of 'the homeless mind'.[9] The public disciplines in which people share have each their own scheme of values, but none of them could or do claim ultimate importance. In the private world autonomy is rife, and ultimate values can be whatever you make them, but here there is no public sharing. Private values are for private indulgence only.

These changes in culture over the last two centuries call in question the perceptions of the reformation period when it made sense to see the priestly service of all the baptised as a publicly recognised activity taking place in the public sphere. At that time it was possible to represent a public office as a vocation under God, to be carried out with godly virtue and godly motives. In the public sphere of our own time it is questionable whether godliness of any kind is either sought or perceived, or whether it is responsive to the Christian conscience in any way at all.

Take, for example, the position of a Christian bureaucrat. Bureaucracies work by dividing up the elements of an administrative process among a number of functionaries, allocating to each one only a limited competence.[10] Personal scope is reduced: predictability is gained. Certain predetermined needs can always be met, rights acknowledged, demands complied with. The process takes on an abstract pattern. It does not matter who they are that operate it, provided they are efficient, and it does not matter who the clients are provided they can supply the required information. The aim is to achieve a human process which is proof against humanity, against likes and dislikes, against moods and bribes and boredom. Names become labels attached to pieces of paper which ultimately deliver up a suitably coded message. They are not, nor are they meant to be, heard as the most precious coinages of human speech.

Now if we in our personal particularity cannot really enter into the bureaucratic process, what is the prospect for God? If a Christian bureaucrat were to complain that his faith seems to make no difference to the way he does his job it could be said in response that the job was designed precisely to prevent that kind of difference. The religion of those who operate the system ought not to affect the system at all. If they operate it a little more conscientiously, that is no real difference, since conscientious cooperation is assumed, and is equally valuable whether it is sustained by faith, by fear or by dullness.

Bureaucracy deliberately minimises the scope of human responsibility, but modern society as a whole, perhaps inadvertently, does so too. It is true that certain people are believed to hold highly responsible positions, but it is very hard to determine the degree of *moral* responsibility in this. A responsible financier, to take another example, will be someone who can be trusted with his client's money, who knows the ways of the market, who is good at making predictions, and can maximise the return. Responsibility here is made up of technical competence and loyalty to certain interests. It would be a quite different kind of responsibility that decided that if these interests were opposed by other interests, then justice or love should be called in to arbitrate between them. There is very small likelihood that anyone who showed an inclination to such behaviour would ever be given the chance to display it.

'How can I be a Christian at work?' is a common question today. It is partly a question about individual morals. Christians may feel pressed by communal forces to tell lies and neglect personal obligations. Yet even if these troubles were eliminated, and there was no question of compromising anyone's personal integrity, the larger problem would remain. 'How can I be a Christian?' means something more than, 'How can I avoid individual corruption?' It means, also, 'How can I commit myself morally to the processes I share in when they are themselves without morality?' It is a question born of the recognition that the assumptions and goals of public corporations are not, except accidentally, the same as those of Christian faith and that the individual Christian working within them is virtually impotent to make any difference to them. A concern for individual integrity here, though not unworthy, is still a retreat to the last trench that can be defended in a painfully exposed field. It is a lapse from the universal priesthood of humanity.

We are dealing here with a problem of definition – not the question of what definition to employ, but of how that definition came to take hold of people's minds. In one sense religion is defined as private because people think of it in that way, but in another it is defined as private by the necessities that operate in public life and which are themselves non-religious. If the ultimate controls in that sphere are economic and technological, since economics and technology are so plainly essential to the whole enterprise that no one can quarrel with them, then faith cannot hope to be its true self except in private. And as long as that remains true no amount of individual faith can redeem society. Society has been placed beyond the reach of the individual will.

Recent political experience bears witness to this. The vote has never been so widely distributed, yet people feel alienated from politics, and cynical about the claims of politicians whether to be or not to be responsible for the course of events. There have been a number of world leaders in recent years who have personally, and no doubt sincerely, professed the Christian faith yet whose policies have been quite as demonic in execution as those of professed atheists. It is hardly contestable that the personal preference of most people in the world is for nations to be at peace with one another, with the threat of nuclear catastrophe removed, and yet the weight of this personal desire seems to make no difference at all to the military planning of their governments.

It is a mental crucifixion just to contemplate these things, and it has been totally crucifying for some of those who have actively challenged the situation at public level. The power of impersonal processes is very great to crush individuals who challenge them with any pretence of effectiveness.

It can be objected that the picture presented here is excessive in its despair, and that there are plenty of experiences to contradict it. It would be astonishing if it were not so, since no social tendency can be more than a tendency. Nevertheless, the tendencies described here are so characteristic of modern times, and can be traced through so many levels of experience that no anecdotal evidence of contraries can come as more than the possibility of a challenge to them.

The natural reaction of a modern Western Christian to the progress of secularity in the world may be to thank God that at least in the ark of the church there remain a faith and a hope that have not been overwhelmed by the flood, which, if anything, stand out more clearly than ever. On reflection, though, he or she may notice that the ark is borne up by the flood, carried by its currents, and not at all menaced by it. The church and its members are not outside modern society, their consciousness is deeply affected by it, and their religious behaviour may be as much a collusion with it as a challenge to it. Let us consider here how the secular tendencies we have described can act upon church life and shape it to their ends.

2. Consequences for the Church

(a) The Triviality of Faith

Faith does not have to have lost its fervour to be trivial. If it ceases to engage with things that matter that is enough. The sense that it has done so surfaces regularly in Christian gatherings. Words like *piety* and *spirituality* are used apologetically. The activities they denote seem to be a misdirection of human potential, not its fulfilment. They call for the engagement of the heart to God, but not the kind of heart you can put into all you do. The soul of which they speak seems insubstantial, elusive; it fails to appear, outside the closet. The Christian is brought into the courts of heaven and assured of the grace of eternal life – and nothing, one might say, could be less trivial than that – yet the reign of the King of heaven is so hard to discern outside the sanctuary that one is moved to ask which is real and which is illusion, the inside or the outside.

This kind of split, between soul and body, sanctuary and society, private and public, is totally inimical to the Christian tradition of faith. It means that God and human experience have been ripped apart. All that is left is 'religious experience' – something that combines the highest claims with the weakest credentials. However much believers may profess their dependence on God they are menaced by the feeling that, in reality – the reality of which everyday life is the standard – God has come to depend upon them.

One way out of this dilemma is to adopt the standards of everyday reality and to proclaim the effectiveness of faith in terms society can recognise. Prayer can become a form of self-cultivation, orientated to tranquillity, the conservation of personal energy, poise. Worldly success can be taken as a measure of divine favour. Signs and wonders may be invoked as a testimony, which even the world can receive, that God is powerful in the way the world understands power. Conversion can be seen as a form of individual therapy, a deliverance from anxiety and restraint, a means of handling dissociation in the personality. Here the criteria of what 'works' and the goals pursued are so far akin to secular criteria and goals that the difference between these and other pragmatic activities can only be sustained by mystification – what we are doing is of the Holy Spirit. What you do is of the devil.

(b) The Introversion of the Church

If we were asked to use sociological criteria alone to devise a religion for secular society, everything would point to the need for an introverted church. As the public world becomes unable to respond materially to religious convictions, the church should confine itself to private concerns. It should present itself as an organiser of leisure activity, a haven of comfortable personal fellowship, an answer to the individual's need for dependence. Its cosmic aspiration should be other-worldly, and its concept of human nature individualistic. Because its other-worldliness will be in sharp contrast to everyday assumptions, a certain sense of separateness, of opposition to the world, will serve the needs of group cohesion. The ideal member – whether the ideal is realisable or not – will belong heart and soul to the church, will devote all his or her time to it, share its ideology implicitly, and hold everything that does not sustain this commitment in fear and contempt. There will be a clear and continuous boundary between what is of the church, and what is not of it, and meetings upon this boundary between insider and outsider will always be tinged with antagonism, however warmly the invitation to come in may be intended.

Of course, even in this inventive age the invention of religions is not quite proper. Better to adopt a tradition whose authority has already been established, making the adaptation as unobtrusive as possible. One way of achieving this would be to represent the new state of the church as a recovery of its original and uncompromised state – revolution by tradition[11] – and so to stigmatise residual, unadaptable parts of church life as a lapse from the original intentions of its founder.

Even if the modern Christian Church has not yet reached this state, does it not show the power of these tendencies? Whether we advert to the gradual shift from communal to associational types of organisation, to the tightening up of sacramental disciplines, to the way most successful reform movements develop a sectarian character, to disgruntlement with institutions and the exaltation of personal encounter, it can hardly be denied that the modern church is sorely tempted to turn in upon itself, and is, in various ways, responding to the temptation. And introversion has one vast advantage in a hostile world, it allows religion to continue as fullblooded religion. The error is to think that in this way it resists the growth of secularisation. A distinction has to be made, and can hardly be made too sharply, between secularisation and secularism. Secularism is opposed to religion. Secularisation is perfectly tolerant of it, provided only that it keep to its own assigned sphere, in the private world.

Jürgen Moltmann writes[12] of the way the church can play a perfectly acceptable palliative role in a society which in no way shares its ultimate conviction. In the world of the 'homeless mind', people feel that their personal value is ignored. They are deprived of fellowship, and their feelings are discounted. By contrast the church provides precisely what public life denies – warmth, immediacy, love. People's struggles with destiny are taken seriously, the need for personal acceptance is met, the constraints of social-role definition can be set aside. Personality is allowed to count within a protected zone against the forces of depersonalisation.

Ironically, the impersonal processes are not at all challenged by this. Rather the contrary. If people are frustrated, frayed and disappointed by their experience of the public world, it makes for efficiency that they should have something to go to which will soothe them, redirect their energies to more accessible goals, and compensate them in their sense of loss. A church which does these things has a clear social function – to neutralise the acids of public life so far as they diminish public effectiveness. It may not operate as an agent of society in the sense in which industrial concerns and government departments are agents of society, but it can expect tolerance and even approval as long as it sticks to its role.

(c) The Ecclesiastical Seduction of the Laity

The way of life of the introverted church may be a distortion of the gospel, but it allows the church to build up confidence and share it with its members. The satisfactions of that life are palpable. People are grateful for them. Public attitudes to faith are sufficiently equivocal to make faith itself shine out like a beacon of certainty, even when it is absurd. The introverted church can demand and get a very high degree of loyalty from its members. Even the world assures them that they are free, responsible individuals, but here alone that freedom seems to have met an object worthy of its choice.

There is then, nothing particularly remarkable about the way many members of the modern laity occupy themselves more in church affairs, are more articulate about their beliefs, and show a deeper conviction of Christian truth than their predecessors did. This would follow in any case from the heightened sense of autonomy in the private sphere, and the sharper separation of that sphere from the public. There is no need to see it as a mighty work of God stirring himself against the forces of unbelief. Insofar as it merely reflects the distorted perspective of the introverted church it cannot be used to justify that introversion. It does, however, have a drastic effect on the inner dynamics of church life. Where these tendencies are at work, the laity are far more ecclesiastics than they would have been elsewhere. Church membership as such has become their vocation, and whatever they do in the rest of society is wholly secondary, or remains only as an embarrassment they would like to be free of. The symbols of faith – and these are understood to point away from the world and not into it – are taken to embody the whole of truth; one must be occupied in them day and night.

It is against that perception that we must evaluate movements to recover the ministry of the church for the laity. Such movements are both necessary and inevitable. The church has a right and duty to expect *ministerium*, service, from every Christian, and now, in a time of rapid change, it badly needs a new way of engaging its lay members with that expectation. It is a way that they, for the most part will have to discover for themselves, since they know their own situation best. New conditions of life and the passage of time throw up new requirements and expose the weakness of old remedies. It will no longer serve to think of the laity as essentially passive before their clergy, saying *amen* to someone else's prayer, taking on trust someone else's teaching. But it will not do to let movements in society, reflecting all the distortions of that society, propose the new solution, even if it comes tricked out with tags from the Bible. Pastoral theology has to look at developments in Christian sentiment as part of the situation to be met, not simply as answers to the predicament. We are warned that the selection and interpretation of texts tends to reflect the interests of the interpreters, and the first steps of faith away from self-interest are steps of suspicion. Is it, perhaps, because a self-consciously activist church is making the selection that the frenetic tendency of 1 Corinthians, chapter 12 is stressed rather than the structure of authority within which it is written, or that a piece of pseudo-Luther – the priesthood of all believers – is preferred to Luther's plain stress on the worldly vocation of Christians? Certainly, other choices could reflect other interests, and the pretence to neutrality is not easily supported, but need Christians always be as shameless as they are in advocating their own cause?

Priesthood is the impossible vocation, and if the laity are laying claim to the priesthood which is inescapably theirs then it is that impossibility which they are offering themselves for. This is not the way in which so much talk about lay ministry goes, with its stress on gifts, competence, equipment and training. Such things have never proved decisive where priesthood itself is at stake. At most they provide a way forward – they shape a Christian's vocation towards the moment when nothing will be of any use but sheer humanity and the consciousness of God.

Luther saw the priest's characteristic action as a bodily paradigm of the spiritual vocation of every Christian – a prayerful setting forth of the glory of God to all, in humble self-dedication to the point of sacrifice. The movement towards introversion in the church misses that. It thinks of the priest as characteristically within and about the church. To share his or her ministry is to be within and about it too. As the movement develops in this direction, confusion grows. The priest's is the template on which the laity's calling is to be modelled, and from that point of view, cannot be eliminated. Yet as the laity are drawn more and more into the ecclesiastical establishment, it begins to seem that laity and clergy are no longer collaborators in the same cause, but rivals for the same space. To say that this will not do is not (at least necessarily) to say that the clergy should be left in undisputed possession of the church. It is to question the picture of the church, turned in upon itself and anxious about its location in the world, which is the undisclosed foundation of the whole development. It is not accidental that as the church takes on a novel shape, determined by the structure of secularisation and not by its own inner genius, a crisis develops for its ordained ministers. A church which has closed the doors on society and become a religious association neither needs nor is a priesthood. Priesthood has its place only in the interplay of society and the sacred, or in Christian terms, God and the human world, and once it cuts loose from that it is lost. We need a recovery of priestly confidence but not, as may be imagined, for the sake of the ordained ministry alone. If ordained ministers are aware of a loss of confidence in their office, a loss which others feel as much as they do themselves, it arises from the sensitivity and representative character of their position. It is upon them that the doubts and misgivings, and the resentment of the church at its own drift away from reality, are projected. They feel in themselves, and in the kind of expectations they meet in others, the predicament of the whole, of laity as well as clergy, unbelievers as well as faithful. A recovery of priestly confidence, then, is needed as much for the sake of the laity as for the clergy, for the sake of the church, and for the sake of humankind. Ultimately what is at stake is whether or not it is true that the Lord is King, and that the earth may be glad thereof, that God remains universally responsible and universally sovereign.

It is the task of Christian priesthood to affirm that the Lord is King even where that truth is ignored, or found meaningless, or denied, and that task leads inexorably towards the point at which all these negative responses are most palpable, the point of death. Modern technological culture tries to eliminate the sense of death as it eliminates the sense of God. It remains, as it was to Eliot in the 1940s, the culture of 'the silent funeral, nobody's funeral for there is no one to bury'.[13] Yet (of course!) death continues to happen, and it still needs interpretation, and while society may cover over and eliminate the fact of death, death cannot be adequately interpreted apart from the experience of society. As someone approaches death, whether proximately or remotely, certain questions are inevitable: what have I done, whom have I met, what deliverance from the isolation of my own defences have I known, and with what quality of love, of sharing, of common purpose sustained in the face of hardship and absurdity have I offered myself to others? Here the compartmentalising of life is perceived in its real tragedy, as men and women try to see their life whole, and find it impossible to do so; as they recognise that in the historical world they were reduced to anonymous cyphers, and only apart from history did they experience some fragmentary achievement.

Healing can occur at this point, and the life that must end can also be brought to completion, only if death itself carries with it a grace of restoration, only if it presents itself as an act of trust in a faithful Creator. Priesthood has an obvious function to fulfil here, as it interprets what has been and what is to be, and presents the tokens of grace, but it is not the primary function. That is fulfilled by the dying person who somehow has to gather up all that he or she has become through life and hand it over to God in a good death.

When a priest has said what is given to be said at that time and has touched the dying body in significant ways, and gone, he or she can reflect on this experience and let it modify, so far as it will, the prospect of his or her own death; but at that moment it is the person ministered to who dies, and so 'makes the sacrifice complete'.[14] Priesthood interprets human experience, and in a substantial way modifes it, but it is those who avail themselves of priesthood who have the experience. Priesthood is nothing if it is not constructively engaged with humanity as such.

Here we may return to the eucharistic pattern of church life which was typical of the earliest centuries – the eucharist as an action in which everyone took part, each according to his or her office. The position of the laity here, it has to be acknowledged, is equivocal. If the eucharistic assembly is seen as something closed off from the world, and its priesthood is distributed among its members in a complete hierarchical order, then it is clear that the laity come at the bottom of the hierarchy, that they represent nothing more than the ground upon which the pyramid rises. Everyone else has a specified function to perform within or for the congregation. The laity simply are the congregation, the part that can remain unspecified. Only if the eucharistic assembly is open, in its fundamental intention, to everyone who is human, and only if the laity are seen as the definitive representatives of humanity, can we say that the laity's function is 'basic' to the whole, that without it nothing can take place, and that it is the transformation of human experience as they experience it that the celebration intends.

Now we know that, at least over a certain period, the eucharistic celebration took place within closed doors, and the unbaptised were excluded from it. Much as we can understand why, in a dangerous world which was only too ready to misinterpret what it knew about Christians, the church preferred its most characteristic action to remain secret, we can be glad that the process of introversion has not yet revived the *disciplina arcani*, and that in principle the doors once opened have not been closed again. A church that meets within closed doors is a church that thinks of itself as complete in itself, and its only concern with those whom it perceives as 'outside' is to invite them in to share its own completeness. But what if the truth points the other way – that it is the church which is incomplete and it needs to work to unite itself with humankind as such to become complete? Then its eucharist is not to be reduced to a piece of arcane piety, the privilege of initiates. It is deprived of its glory if it does not acknowledge that 'the whole earth is full of God's glory' and if it does not mediate the glory of God back to the whole earth.

Clergy and laity have mutual responsibilities here, in preventing this fresh closure of the church against the world. There will be times when out of a clearheaded perception of the godlessness of our culture, Christian laymen and women will seek to broaden the defences and close the doors. At such times the task of priests will be to keep the church aware of its own incompleteness. To do this they will have to take on the function of irritants, remembering that however strong their solidarity with the rest of the church they are also, by vocation, 'from outside',[15] the persons who represent

God's own detachment from his church. They are of the church, but socially and psychologically, they cannot be its priest if they get locked into it, and so lend the authority of their office to its illusion of completeness.

But there will also be times when priests, responding to the definition of their office that modern culture imposes, will become over-zealous for the church's claims upon its members, will portray a God who is incapable of breaking out of the round of devotion. At these times the laity, who know at first hand what life is really like, will need to press the claims of that kind of life to recognition, to judgement and grace and blessing. And they will need to do this, not by claiming to be too busy or too tired for church activities, but by asserting the claim of God in the things which tire and busy them.

Priesthood takes place within a sacramental transaction that requires at least two participants, two parties in conversation. The grace of this sacrament is a meeting between God and humankind, and the matter of the sacrament is also a meeting in which one participant is priestly and the other, not lay, but human. Christ is not the redeemer of ecclesiastical life, but of human nature, human endeavour and playfulness, human suffering and sin. Those who minister Christ, even though they minister in the sanctuary, have to have their eyes set upon these more distant objectives. Distant from the sanctuary, they may be, but near enough to anyone who is prepared to acknowledge their common membership of the human race, and not to hide from their own flesh.

CHAPTER NINE

Priestly Askesis Today

For every high priest, being taken from among human beings, is appointed for them in things pertaining to God . . .

Hebrews 5.1

1. Learned Obedience

A pragmatic culture defines people by their usefulness – by the power they exercise and the things they do. A political culture which exalts democracy, even when the forms of democracy are patently manipulated, looks for leaders who can concentrate the popular will. A system of organisations competing for survival commits itself again and again to the hands of managers. A world in which military priorities determine the ends, and military paradigms determine the means, expects its managers to operate strategically, to set objectives, to mount campaigns and to do battle with opponents.

Priesthood is something different from all these, except at a very late stage of its unfolding, when its own inner vocation leads it, temporarily and accidentally, to take on the colours and patterns of the world it serves. In an organised world priests too have to organise. They have to manage themselves, if nothing and no one else, and they have to adopt techniques and borrow metaphors from the experts in these matters if they are to do it acceptably. It becomes tempting, then, to think that these things make up the substance of priesthood, the only characteristic difference in the work of priests being that they lead, manage and organise religious groups rather than secular ones. It is tempting, that is, for priests themselves – a moral assault on their priesthood which they have to recognise and resist, a denial of the new world to which their lives have been dedicated, of the new birth by which that world is entered.

The training of a priesthood, then, is only accidentally a matter of acquiring techniques, or procedures, or answers to anticipated questions. It is primarily ascetical. It requires the acceptance of an inner discipline, of a process of formation, in response to a call that lays hold upon men and women at the heart of their personalities. It means taking the common Christian disciplines, prayer, repentance and active faith, with entire seriousness, and not only on one's own behalf but as someone in whom the needs and aspirations of others are focussed and represented. It means letting God have his way, at the point where ideas are questioned, attitudes are challenged, feelings are exposed in their confusion, motives in their immaturity. It means the acquisition of an instinct, a taste for God.

No one, I imagine, would deny that something of this kind is important for a minister of the church. I want to go beyond words like important, though, even words like necessary, fundamental, essential. All of these may be satisfied if an ascetical dimension is acknowledged, or if askesis – spiritual formation – is seen as a component of a man's or woman's response to the call to priesthood. After all, the askesis of the athletes from whom we borrow the term is a preliminary to the games. It refers to exercises undertaken by athletes in order to get them fit for the real business of their life, competition. But this too is one of the ways in which priesthood is different, in which borrowed language has to be reinterpreted if it is not to be misleading. For a priest, askesis is not a preparation for ministry but ministry itself. It provides for the beginnings which come to us again and again in Christian ministry, but also for every continuation and completion. Priests minister, not, at root, by what they do, but by what they are, what they symbolise, what they show forth. Priestly formation then, is not a goal to be attained before one goes on to do the work of priesthood. It is the work itself and the work of priesthood is known to be priestly because it has this direction. Properly understood, all Christian action is laid under the definition 'you are a royal priesthood, a holy nation, to show forth the excellencies of the one who called you' (1 Pet. 2.9). Ascetical theology, not management or strategy, is the basic pastoral science.

2. Taken from among human beings in things pertaining to God

The phrase is applied to Christ in Hebrews, but it applies to all priests, including Christian ones. The priests are likely to be embarrassed. The embarrassment has to be borne. Some think they may diminish it by diminishing the claims made for their office. They may think that by stressing the aspect of servanthood in their calling, being there for the sake of *others*, to affirm *their* gifts, enable *their* ministry, release *their* energies, they can somehow climb down from the pinnacle upon which the idea of priesthood places them. They fail to see that such servanthood derives all its value, its effectiveness in social relations and its power as an example of humility, from its being the servanthood of the priest, the person who acts for humankind in things pertaining to God. Individual priests may deny that it is so, whole parties may try to sustain a sub-culture in which the priestliness of priesthood is systematically denied. But people who have not experienced the embarrassment, as well as many who have and still do, know that the denial is false. Even when it is respected, even when in a certain way it is believed and acted upon, it is known to be false, because it is the priestly authority behind the denial which wins it acceptance.

The priest's institutional function is to speak and act in God's name, to play God's part for him, to occupy the social space that humankind leaves empty for God to fill but which God (it seems) insists on having filled by people like ourselves. That can remain clear, attested by common sense and required by that audacity without which theology is impossible, in the face of a good deal of modest understatement and deliberate obfuscation or contradiction. If priesthood really is what it appears to be, the act of God in a human institutional context, then a certain crazy syntax in the statements it makes on its own behalf is hardly to be wondered at. 'He that believes in me,' says Jesus in John 12.44 'does not believe in me'. The illogicality of the statement can be avoided only if the situation it points to can be avoided; that is, if people come to faith in a way which contradicts Jesus and his peculiar calling, or if they do not believe at all.

The embarrassment has to be borne, but its nature has to be understood. The anxiety lies, not in the risk of claiming more than can be sustained, but in the risk of permitting a claim that defies comprehension to become the object of complacency, to be set down as a mere matter of fact. Priesthood, like all social institutions, aspires to the status of a matter of fact, but unlike other social institutions, not a 'mere' matter of fact. Its social function requires it to be permanently perplexing. The risk God takes in acting through human priests – perhaps we might say, in committing himself to humankind at all – is that he will then appear as a tame God, whose power has been passed into the hands of human beings to dispose of as they will. Once this happens – or rather is believed to have happened – then the clamour is bound to arise to have God released again into his original wild state, free to act apart from institutions, apart from humanity. But the truth is not that beyond the tame God of religious institutions there is a free God trying to break through, nor that beyond the predictable God of priesthood there is an elusive God who must be sought by another route. The God who chooses to draw near through priesthood is himself the free, elusive, holy God. That is the immensity of the claim that has to be made for priesthood, and no one who allows himself to act in God's name can avoid making it. When Paul exclaims 'who is sufficient for these things?' (2 Cor. 2.17), he speaks not out of a sense that mere virtue, mere strength, mere skill, mere knowledge would restore equilibrium to his disturbed conscience, but out of confusion at finding himself to be, in his own person, a touchstone of salvation or damnation in others. This confusion is the heart of apostleship.

Paul's 'who?' can only refer to God. He is saying 'God save me!' – save me, not *from* my calling, nor even in the course of my calling, but in the calling itself which seems to carry the certainty of hell in its very nature if God does not adopt it as his own.

That is why, as a priest, I must pray. In my accessibility to others I am a sign of the elusive and holy God. My business is to point beyond myself, and I can do this only if I live from beyond myself, if I receive my work, my calling, my very self from God, if I allow it to be said of me, as it must be said of the Holy Spirit, that I am always gift and never possession.

Prayer of this kind has no object in view but to acknowledge God. It does not try to make use of him. There is an amusing irony – whether intended or not is hard to say at this distance in time and culture – in the passage where Ezra writes that having boasted of God's protection he had to resort to prayer and fasting in order to induce God to conform to the scheme prepared for him (Ezra 8.22). Less amusing, almost pathetic, is the sight of Christians concentrating the power of their prayers upon their own acts of ministry, as though the duty of praying for humankind can only be discharged by prayer for their own success. Traditionally the church's expectation of its priests has moved in a different direction. Saints have been honoured for their power as intercessors, but the ordinary priest is not called to power but to regularity, to the unemphatic recitation of the daily office. For the office is neither eloquent nor magical in its selection of material. Rather it covers and explores with little discrimination every sentiment, every aspiration, that has ever been expressed among the people of God, whether good or bad, penetrating or jejune. It is, as the Bible itself is, nothing more than humanity before God, and priests are called upon simply to set themselves in the midst of that humanity, and with it to acknowledge that God is God, gracious, humble, present in his hiddenness, worth the time it takes.

The daily office has no true climax. It is never, as we experience it, a complete act, since every offering of morning or evening prayer looks onwards to its augmentation at the next recitation, the next evening or morning. It moves through cycles that have no end in themselves because the end appointed for them remains at God's disposal alone. That is not to say that the office cannot be 'done well', as it often is, even as a public event, but part of its achieved goodness is the sense of something more to come, just as a vigil looks forward to a feast.

Priests need to experience their priesthood as vigilants, not as feasters. In the practical outworking of their ministry there is a good deal that strives against that. They may feel themselves at a loss if they cannot point to their own experience as an encouragement to others. In a society which increasingly lacks any common perception of the meaning of repentance, and which reduces God's universal love to tolerant indifference, the lack of obvious examples of what we mean by faith in Christ can be felt very acutely. The next stage, which may seem to offer the only way ahead, is a sense of duty to embody Christianity, to know what we are talking about by being it. Without assured progress in wisdom and power, how can anyone dare to minister to the simple and the weak! 'He saved others, himself he cannot save', remains a reproach, it seems, even if Christ crucified has taken it upon himself.

But the truth is that any deliberate attempt to present oneself as an example of grace in action is a betrayal of the gospel we seek to commend. The mystery of grace is not that weakness is replaced by strength, or sin by righteousness, but that in our weakness we are strong, and, while remaining sinners, justified. Of course, it is true that the gospel promises perfection but it does not promise either instant or gradual perfection. Paul had seen sufficiently well how scandalous the claim to perfection can be as to take up the opposite position himself, that of the one for whom all was yet to come. 'Forgetting what lies behind, and reaching forward to what lies ahead, I seek to grasp that for which Christ has grasped me' (Phil. 3.12). That is all a priest, or any Christian, can really claim to know in experience: that he or she has been grasped. Priests bear witness to a promise which has never failed them, even though (so far as they know) they have never really responded to it themselves.

3. In all things like unto his brothers and sisters

Whether we are thinking of Christ specifically, or of priesthood in general, the priest who is separated for God has to remain, and indeed become, wholly involved in the life of humankind, not becoming detached from human things, but making them the principal material of the task. The task of the priest is to be really human, like all other human beings. A simplistic understanding of christology, applied analogically to priesthood, might take this to mean no more than physically human. The great christological formulae are easily interpreted in purely physical terms, as though Jesus represents the union of only abstract divine and human natures, and so mediates the presence of God to humankind without that presence entering in any concrete way into human experience. But any careful reading of the Fathers will show that christological formulae only come alive in the face of serious questions about the human experience of Christ, and that is the perspective which is wholly to the fore in Hebrews. It is not human nature, in the abstract, but human experience which Jesus has to enter into fully if he is to be qualified for priesthood. And, significantly, that experience can be summarised as suffering. It is most itself at the point at which its meaning and value to us is most elusive, and our lack of power over our own health and balance is most exposed.

It is hardly surprising that the history of christology has worked itself out against a subconscious desire in the Church to diminish Christ's humanity, to deny that he would, like us, have to face real temptation, real uncertainty, a real constitutional imbalance in his experience of himself. It is only gradually that Christians recognise these things in themselves. If, then, we say that the human nature of a Christian priest has to be affirmed, we enter into contradiction within the very milieu in which priesthood is exercised. Religion is a powerful instrument for those who want to deny or reject aspects of their own humanity. It carries within itself a deep-rooted conviction that those who are central to religious practice are human only in a sanitised, expurgated sense. Ordination to priesthood, like conversion of any kind, can be attractive because it promises an end to the constitutional imbalance, because it defines as unacceptable those parts of our own experience which perplex and dismay us, and pledges their abolition. This kind of selective self-identity in the priest can be sought, not only by the priests for their own sake, but by all those who want to look to them for comfort with themselves. The truth exemplified in Christ, and articulated in Hebrews in terms of priesthood, is the exact opposite. It is not by the excision of human capacities but by comprehending them in God's name that any human being can become capable of mediating the presence of God to humankind.

An attempt to list the excisable capacities is likely to begin with sex, and this priority, though not the excision, may be justified. It is within our experience of sexuality that most of us are confronted with our own capacity for unpredictable desires and amazing initiatives, that we catch glimpses of ourselves that are hardly continuous with the reputation we seek to maintain in other ways. Once this is seen, sex can be recognised as the most obvious, and perhaps the most trivial, of those energies within ourselves which, as they emerge, challenge our sense of having established our own truth and being secure enough to live within it. From the standpoint of that truth insisting on its own finality, these signals from a richer world can look only like a threat of chaos. Redemption then seems to lie in escaping to a place of safety where the threat is no longer felt, not in allowing the threatening energy to present itself where it can be affirmed, interpreted and consecrated. Yet priesthood, certainly Christian priesthood with its conviction that everything is God's creation, is in the business of interpreting and consecrating. Insofar as religion excludes that possibility, Christian priesthood has to transcend it.

A priesthood which is shaped by the knowledge of Christ will be a priesthood which aims to become like, to stand with, others in their suffering, perplexity and fear. Its root virtue is compassion. None can help to open up a situation to God who do not perceive that they are in that situation themselves, who cannot acknowledge their own shame and guilt, grief and perplexity when they offer themselves, in God's name, as a resource to those who share in those conditions.

That means that priests' experience of themselves, and the awareness they bring to that experience, is an element in their dealings with others which can never be absent, nor ever should be. Their ability to relate the experience to the grace of God is conditional upon their ability to read it aright, to comprehend it in its complexity and in all its disturbing aspects, and this is impossible if they have imposed a brittle and naive assurance upon their experience of themselves. Jesus is able to act representatively in the meeting of God with humanity, not because he looks human but because he feels it, is aware of himself with a truly human consciousness, though with a lucidity that only faith in a loving creator can sustain. And every priest, given a share in that representative task, has to aim at the same lucidity.

Modern insights into the psychology of interpersonal relationships may help us here. The Latinate *compassion* and the Grecian *sympathy* both mean, at root, suffering with the other. This is not a comfortable idea, nor does it carry much pragmatic value. To feel the agony of another as one's own is, conceivably, to share that person's disability, to be as much in need of rescue as he or she is. Better it may seem to restrict sympathy to nothing more than a benevolent interest considerate of the other's distress, as reflected in one's own outward demeanour, and then offer oneself to them, not as like them but as helpfully unlike them, strong where they are weak.

But the practice of psychotherapy and counselling has introduced us to a new term, *empathy*, which is significantly distinct. Empathy is suffering *in* the other, that is recognising one's own condition in the condition of the other. Empathy is not felt in the guts, as an involving affection that thrusts one into identity with the afflicted. It arises in the active imagination, discerning, recognising the resonances between one's own experience and that of the other. It requires, not identity of condition, but a sense of analogy within the manifold experience of people, in spite of the limitless variation in the way the themes and motifs can be combined. It is not saying, or even being entitled to say, 'I know exactly what you mean'. It is the state of being able to suggest a meaning which the sufferer can recognise as their own.

Both of these ideas, sympathy and empathy, contribute to priestly compassion (though of course neither can contribute to the richness of the concept if it is not kept distinct from the other). The idea of empathy shows us how Jesus could be made 'in all things' like to us, and how priests who derive their vocation from him can at least approximate to that condition. The claim is not being made that Jesus suffered or enjoyed every experience possible to humankind, but that in his life and death taken together, and in the faith that informed both, there is a paradigmatic richness which, with sensitivity, can illuminate every human experience. Priests have to ask themselves how their own awareness of the human situation can carry something of the same quality, and help them really to hear and see what people are saying when they wrestle inarticulately with their own experience of life. At the same time the fact that Jesus actually died, and did not simply formulate concepts of death at second hand, points to a continuing and drastic demand for sympathy as well. Priests who undertake to work with people in their necessity are tacitly giving a pledge to enter into their necessity with them. The more confusing and disorientating their state, the more the priests too may have to let go of the tried and tested certainties, and so prove themselves as ministers of faith.

Empathy and sympathy, defined in this way, can have a multitude of concrete forms, simply because human need and aspiration is itself so diverse. There is, though, one general condition which touches everyone in the modern world, and which calls out for compassionate understanding from every modern priest. This world, at least in its public aspect, is a world without faith, a world without God. Unless priests are able to enter imaginatively into that faithless and godless condition they will be useless, as priests, to most people. Even believers, even priests themselves, are in their cultural formation deeply imbued with unbelief, and, if they cannot recognise this, acknowledge it and seek to make it lucid to themselves, then they are trapped within their own defences and cannot pretend that their so-called ministry is anything but a way of serving themselves. For example, a Christian woman, in her employment, her friendships, her marriage and motherhood, her provision for her family, her concern for its future, will for the most part order her life and feelings along lines which everyone like her in society follows, whether Christian or not. In one situation after another the common prudence which shapes her actions has itself been shaped by a culture which excludes faith, whose ends are, apparently, attainable without it. Modern priestly ministry, to be modern, has to begin by confronting this truth, and then go on to bring a lovingly fascinated interest to it. The alternative is to demonise it, and so to close one's heart against every expression of it.

Some of the most powerful expressions of it come from those founding fathers of the behavioural sciences, Freud, Marx, and – now that socio-biology has emerged – Darwin. If priests, in their training or afterwards, cannot comprehend what these men were saying, can only distort or reject them, they show their incapacity to minister in a genuinely modern world. That is not to say that these men were correct, either in general or in detail. Their correctness, in this perspective, is irrelevant. The point is that they give theoretical expression to perceptions of the way things are in the world that run far deeper than the intellect and which are woven into the public imagination in ways which precede any familiarity with their writings, and which have developed strength in proportion to the loss of a shared sense of God's sovereignty in society. If the various psychological and sociological reductions of the sense of God have force, it is because the sense of God itself is experienced, in most social interaction today, in a reduced form. If then we identify the God who is portrayed through this truncated sense with the living God, ruler of creation, and set about defending his image apologetically, as not likely to upset the general run of things at all, we have certainly fallen into idolatry.

The modern priest needs to be a better atheist than the next man or woman, than the comfortable unbeliever whose doubts are not that God may not exist, but that perhaps he may. Modern priests have to have entered with deeper understanding, with clearer eyes, into the absence of God from the modern world. They must know the arguments against God's real existence more accurately, and be able to deploy them better. Without such awareness it cannot be said that they may become in all things like their fellow human beings, that they can meet them where God continually meets them, on their own ground. This finely imagined and experienced atheism is required, not because it represents the ultimate truth nor because it has become a healthier and more advanced form of faith than faith itself, but because it defines the context of most human experience today.

Admittedly, it is possible to await the arrival of other experiences, even to contrive them, at those points in life where cultural continuities are always threatened and sometimes break down. But to do this is to abandon most of the world to the devil. It is to say that the material available is wholly unsuitable for the scheme our God has in mind.

4. In the midst of the congregation

Anthropologically considered, the institution of priesthood assumes an entire society whose priesthood it is. It conforms to a social necessity to bind people together, to articulate their sense of the sacred, and to help them support one another in the face of ultimate fear. Christian theology seems to turn the concept to another use. The priesthood of humanity restored in Christ means the sanctification of all human experience, the abolition of the distinction between the sacred and the secular. Nevertheless, although the anthropological and the theological ideas are different in content, they are not, while time lasts, actually opposed. There is nothing contradictory in the idea that the sacred should witness to its own final dissolution, and it is on this basis that sacral priesthood and Christian priestliness have been reconciled in history. They are reconciled under the cross.

What Christian priesthood cannot let slip is the universal appeal of the cross, or, in other words, its own function as an institution of society. In spite of the ways in which religion has come to be characterised in the modern world as private, individual, occurring in the interstices of social structure, the calling of Christian priesthood is to serve and sanctify the whole life of humankind. Society may not recognise this, but the Christian priesthood must recognise it of itself or lose its *raison d'être.* The God it acknowledges makes this claim upon it. Priesthood is a public function, and must be sustained in the public sphere.

It is here that the individual priest may need to make some finely judged choices, or even simply live with an insoluble dilemma. Schematically, the age of social respect for Christian institutions belongs to the past. The future is 'post-Christian', and in it there is no more perceived significance in Christian clergy than in the leaders of any voluntary group. But the present – the social-historical present – is not the point at which this past gives way to this future, but the span of experience in which they overlap. One cannot simply declare that the Church has lost all social influence when it clearly has not, and when people are still moved by cultural influences and personal needs to look to it for help. The alienation from reality to which Christians are so liable, of declaring that what ought to be really is, is particularly vicious in this case, first because it distorts Christian perceptions of the honesty of the fragile interest that people still have in the church, and secondly because the 'ought' which is affirmed here is no more than a speculative projection in any case. Those who would like to put the present age down as post-Christian without remainder miss the way in which Christian themes have not merely appeared in human consciousness and then receded from it, but, once lodged there, have undergone successive transformations and so remained part of the inheritance of every culture that has ever opened itself to faith. Or, if that be granted, they conclude without evidence that no further transformation can take place without the loss of its essential Christianity. At the same time it would be futile to deny that the interest that remains *is* fragile, the motivations conventional, weak and confined. The same people, the very same groups, can dismiss the Church as irrelevant on one occasion and demand its services on another, as though their title to those services were not in doubt.

Finding a public way through this situation cannot be easy, since any chosen course may be misunderstood. What can be affirmed, though, is that the way must remain public. The Kingdom of God is not a private matter. A priesthood which seeks the sanctification of the whole of life has to enter fully into the experience of humankind, both private and public, and where old forms of public engagement no longer serve then new forms have to be discovered.

The simplest strategy, if strategy it is, for achieving this seems to be to let existing public ministries develop in whatever way seems to meet current needs. There are severe dangers in this, since reaction to an emergency on the part of those who have not understood it can often exacerbate it. Still, working from its established ministerial patterns of incumbency and chaplaincy, the church has evolved various sector ministries, like those of industrial mission and social responsibility, and forms of non-stipendiary ministry including those in which the minister seeks to work out his or her calling as fully as possible within a secular employment.

There appears to be promise here of an opening towards society, but appearances can deceive. The formal intentions of a sector ministry, or that of a ministry in secular employment, appear to be an affirmation of the secular sphere as the concern of God. We tend to see this in contrast with monasticism or other forms of the religious life which seem to start from a deliberate renunciation of the secular. In fact, more seems to depend on the ascetical instincts which work themselves out in a particular ministry than in its formal constitution. The monastery, in our modern world, becomes increasingly what Kierkegaard saw it to be, the lighthouse from which we take our bearings. Its very distinctiveness gives it a public role. On the other hand, sector ministries can be seen by their practitioners as the base for raids upon a godless world rather than ways of discovering the path of God in that world; and non-stipendiary ministry can become the badge of a sectarian mentality, when associational churches promote their own activists to ordained office, precisely in order to gain recognition for the kind of private religion they embody.

The ambivalence in these developments reflects the modern Christian ambivalence towards the public world. There can be no advance toward a recovery of real priesthood unless the ambivalence is resolved, and the 'public', however dehumanised and oppressed, is acknowledged to be human and capable of redemption. Priesthood must affirm the public world for God's sake, and that will mean affirming the priest's own public status first, as the starting point for priestly ministry, as providing an occasion for ministry, and then beyond that as belonging to the substance of ministry. It is because priests inhabit, suffer from, and contribute to the same world as people in general that they can minister to them there. The priest-worker must learn to speak at all times as both priest and worker; without the status of worker he or she has no real claim to be a priest either. The pressure to swap hats in the course of a conversation or to give secular necessity its victory and reserve spiritual concern for spiritual occasions, has to be steadily resisted.

There is, of course, a built-in tendency in all priesthood to stand back from society. The priest is a separated person, as well as one who belongs intimately to the human race. The problem this poses is that of remaining separate while at the same time deeply involved, and the problem can never be solved perfectly or once and for all. It is quite simply the task and the endurance of a lifetime.

At times the neutrality of the priesthood towards other social institutions has real social value. Bishops, clergy, commissions acting in the church's name, can sometimes address a situation or mediate between parties with an authority which is easier to recognise because they clearly do not stand for any particular interest. There is here, though, no encouragement for those who would keep the church out of all public affairs, since the purpose served by this neutrality is clearly a public one. Theologically, the ground of such a ministry is to be found in the transcendence of God, in his property as judge, and not in any imputed indifference on his part. And just as the transcendent God acts upon the world immanently, the judge reveals himself in grace, so the neutral church has to be a well-informed church, a church that knows through experience and insight what is really at stake in human quarrels and perplexities.

Priesthood arises out of a need to make, or to state, connections. Even on the level of creaturely experience it cannot be an end in itself. The real test of a priesthood is the life of the society it serves, the quality of faith to be experienced within the whole church. Christian priesthood is measured by the demands made in life upon the Christian laity.

The prayer-life, the spirituality, of a Christian priest, therefore, needs at all times to be open to lay experience, and in the end to the experience of all creation. It cannot afford to adopt principles and styles which lay people cannot themselves adopt, however much those principles and styles may be coloured by the peculiar pastoral responsibilities of the priesthood. The idea that the priest does something instead of the laity certainly has no standing, nor the idea that a special spirituality is needed in order to give lustre and prominence to the priest's special calling. There is a certain allure, and some solace to a tender conscience, in the idea that a priest can seek holiness and grace merely through the pastoral duties of priesthood, through preaching and teaching, through leading worship and presiding at the eucharist. The hollowness of this approach is exposed when the same priest finds it impossible to worship seriously under someone else's direction, and when other people's sermons are heard as no more than examples of professional technique. The truth is that everyone, including the ordained Christian, needs to come before God first of all simply as a human being, and the system of prayer and penitence he or she adopts has to retain recognisable roots in ordinary human experience.

There is, to develop a theme we have already noted, a peculiar involution that infects Christian prayer, when events and projects which are essentially acts of worship become themselves the subject of prayer, so that at the furthest limit of this tendency the church finds itself praying for nothing but its own prayer life. Prayers for future services, sermons, evangelistic efforts and other church-centred activities all manifest this tendency for the ecclesiastical heart to become *incurvatus in se*, and to lose its hope and instinct that the whole world shall show forth God's glory.

Compared with these things the prayer of lay Christians who will simply ask God to help them do their daily work, meet their neighbours in a neighbourly way, and acknowledge the common life of the communities they belong to, is a far more profound expression of the Kingdom of God. If priests cannot share in that because their priesthood denies them knowledge of what is really to be observed in such prayer, then already, we can say, their priesthood has atrophied. From it a human being who simply wanted to be human in God's presence would find little or nothing to learn.

Much Christian worship today pretends to be public; a welcome to all is proclaimed from church notice boards. The pretence is exposed when those who come in from the fringe, let alone beyond it, are struck by a clear message that they do not really belong here, they are 'outsiders'. It is not simply that language is obscure, symbols opaque, customs and manners unfamiliar. The same would be true of any tradition of public performance, military, sporting or, to go no further, artistic. The special character of church performances lies in the possibility that the language and symbols available will be used to demonstrate, more clearly perhaps than any other proposition, that those who employ them regard themselves as out of communion with other human concerns. The very firm assertion, on the part of Christian worshippers, that this is where they belong ('We are the Body of Christ') makes it plain to intruders that they do not belong.

Against this largely unconscious tendency in Christian spirituality we need a conscious and deliberate attempt to move in the opposite direction. Against a public but exclusive style of worship we need one that will be largely secret but open in principle to all. Its essential character will be the offering of ordinary human aspirations and needs to God, grief at sin and suffering, sensitivity to the calling of love, dogged responsibility before the truth and the rejection of all bogus absolutions. People who are genuinely hungry and thirsty after righteousness will be able to recognise those who follow such a spirituality. Outside such recognitions it may have no way of declaring itself. That will not matter, since self-declaration will be no part of its concern.

In this exploration of priestly ascetical discipline today there may be a good deal that seems contradictory. As a priest I am to pray the daily office, but like a human being. I am to carry out public rituals, and yet seek my own humanity in the unritualised confusion of ordinary life. I am to glory in public office, yet draw my spiritual sustenance from habits of recollection sustained in secret. I am to be an expert and a common man. A partial response to that sense of contradiction is to say that the priesthood is a shared calling, and that no single priest is called to everything. I can live vicariously, and without apology, from the gifts and graces of my fellows. But a more fundamental response is to say that priesthood always is contradictory, since it operates at the point in human affairs where the presence of God exposes the contradictoriness of the world. There is no complete integrity held out to human life this side of the cross. The promise that there is integrity and peace beyond the cross can only be spoken here in the language of the cross itself.

5. Made Perfect

But there are two points in every priest's life when prayer about prayer is unavoidable – the entry upon ritual worship and the exit from it. These awkward thresholds call out for a most delicately judged step, call for a style of prayer that recognises its own preliminary or retrospective character. There is a transition to be negotiated, a redirection of intention or emotional impulse to be managed, and the negotiator has to undergo the transition too. It may sound foolish to say, 'Put yourself in the presence of God', when God is (surely?) never absent, but it really is foolish to suppose that God's presence is always recognisable to us, and always in the same way. There is a difference that cannot be eliminated between our everyday controlling apprehension of the world around us and our openness to the immediate address of God in symbolic ritual. If most worshippers accept this and manage the alternation successfully without reflection, that does not mean that it is easy to understand. People alternate between sleep and waking with equally small understanding of what is happening. As priest I do need some understanding since it is my business to help both others and myself through the transitions, and to recognise how the process can be complicated or frustrated by other factors. I am myself a key element in the complex of symbolic media that the worshippers address themselves to, and it is my action which, at least in sign, binds them to it or releases them from it.

It remains a question, though, whether I can bind or release myself. From the time of my ordination, is not my whole life marked by ritual character? How otherwise could I initiate ritual action with others? Nevertheless there is some difference between my role as focal person in the church and my character as a human animal. Rising from sleep, washing, dressing, walking down the road are not in principle anything but banal human acts, even though the walk leads into the vestry and on towards the altar. Our invention of the vestry, though, shows another principle at work as well. Neither secular as perceived by the secular world nor sacred as perceived from the altar, what goes on in the vestry exposes the whole problem of relating the holy to the common, the symbolic to the practical, faith to life. For some the vestry is to be a place of silence where every gesture shares in the liturgical character of the actions it is meant to prepare for. For others, vestries are places for informal business, impromptu staff meetings, friendly and therefore necessary chats with young people, while robes are put on and properties assembled. Only on the brink of ritual must silence be imposed and a prayer be said. And even if robes are dispensed with and properties reduced to a minimum, still as ministers move to their appointed places and take up responsibility for the congregation's conduct, a transition is effected. The denial that sacred and secular stand apart cannot be sustained as long as moments occur which mark the beginning and ending of 'the service', as long as there are people who breathe differently before it starts and when it is over.

For the Christian priest, though, that offer of post-ritual freedom is embarrassing. Christian faith knows a good deal about fresh beginnings, renewed opportunities, but it says nothing encouraging as to moves back, reversions, temporary endings. It makes sense to enter upon God's presence, but it sounds confused and unfortunate to say that the time has come to leave it. We may look for help in the idea of internalisation. The presence which gave itself to us in encounter now abides with us, and is (so to speak) carried out with us when we go. The final blessing of the service imposes the name of God upon the worshippers and commissions them to practise what they have received in symbol. But who can say whether the priest who gives the blessing also receives it? And then comes the vestry prayer.

Muriel Spark in one of her novels draws attention to the Catholic custom of concluding grace after meals with a prayer for the dead, curious, as though we had eaten them. The same prayer is often said in the vestry after the service and even those who feel easy about praying for the dead may wonder why. The priest, dealing in matters of life and death, should know that what the ritual proclaims has its fulfilment in the kingdom of the dead. True, it is also prolonged in the daily lives of the worshippers, and this is part of its own intentionality, but no event within those lives will truly satisfy the promise that was renewed in worship. Christian worship looks for a consummation, and in this world that can only be found in death. The priest's peculiar relation to the worship of humankind forces him or her to recognise that truth, and to appropriate the recognition personally and existentially.

If, for the lay worshipper, ritual ends with dismissal into another mode of faith and holiness, for the priest no such ending is given. You go back to eating and drinking, writing letters and paying bills, but the representative character of your existence keeps even these things in tangential contact with the symbolic, ritual world. Internalisation is not enough. The symbols of God's promise are inscribed upon your body and actions as well as upon your heart. Every action, then, renews the promise to translate the symbol into practice, and demands yet another action. A priest's ministry is never complete in this world. Whatever word I have addressed to another, whatever meaning I have imparted by my sacramental authority and presence, also remains with me. I am in debt to all who have received my ministry to live out, and go on living out, the meaning of what I signified to them. In the nature of Christian hope this offers no conclusion short of the age to come.

I was ordained by Michael Ramsey, who summed up the meaning of Christian ordained ministry in four statements. The first two, drawn from scripture, were used as chapter headings in his greatest book.[1]

'One died for all.'

'Therefore all died!'

The third can be found in the same book, at the conclusion of the chapter on the episcopate.

'And those who possess it will tremble and never boast, for none can say it is "theirs". It proclaims that there is one family of God before and behind them all, and that all die daily in the Body of Him who died and rose.'

The fourth statement was his own death.

Notes

Chapter One

1. See Urban T. Holmes III, *The Priest in Community* (New York, 1978, p. 1) and E. O. James, *The Nature and Function of Priesthood* (London, 1955, p. 13).
2. P. Berger, 'The Problem of Multiple Realities: Alfred Schutz and Robert Musil' in T. Luckmann (ed.), *Phenomenology and Sociology*, Harmondsworth, 1978, p. 360.
3. James, *op. cit.*, 1955, Chapter 4, *Kingship and Priesthood.*
4. My debt to P. Berger and T. Luckmann will be evident here, as elsewhere. See their *The Social Construction of Reality*, Harmondsworth, 1967 and Luckmann, *The Invisible Religion*, New York, 1967.
5. Austin Farrer seems to have coined the phrase – 'a sort of walking sacrament, a token of Christ wherever he is' – while leaving it to others to develop (*A Celebration of Faith*, London, 1970, p. 110).
6. I accept projection as a proper procedure for arriving at analogical concepts of the truth of faith. Alistair Kee in his *Constantine versus Christ* (London, 1982) attempts a massive demolition of Constantinian and post-Constantinian Christianity on the ground that it rests simply on projection. He finds the values of Constantinian Christianity to be simply Constantine's own projected into heaven. Certainly one must seek for criteria as to what a proper projective enterprise might be, but such enterprises are unavoidable. Even to condemn them may simply reflect values which have their locus in political radicalism or in despair, and so conform by simple inversion to the very mechanism which is being condemned.
7. B. C. Ollenburger (*Zion, the City of the Great King*, Sheffield, 1987, pp. 152–155) against the view that the Jerusalem cult of the monarchy provides legitimation for royalist absolutism, shows that, on the contrary, its symbols insist on royal accountability and actually support prophetic critique of royal behaviour.

   Reference to the stories of David and Bathsheba and of Creon and Antigone should make acknowledgement of their treatment in P. Berger, *The Social Reality of Religion*, Harmondsworth, 1973, p. 105 (David) and D. MacKinnon, *Themes in Theology*, Edinburgh, 1987 pp. 110ff (Antigone).
8. J. Moltmann, *The Crucified God*, London, 1974, p. 186.

Chapter Two

1. See E. P. Sanders, *Paul, the Law & the Jewish People*, London, 1985, (p. 199).
2. Cf. F. W. Dillistone, *The Power of Symbols*, London, 1986 (p. 87).
3. I am not now able to say whether these thoughts derive from H. W. Fowler's classic statement, *A Dictionary of Modern English Usage*, Oxford, 1926, pp. 348ff, or from W. Empson's more baroque treatment of the theme, *Seven Types of Ambiguity*, Harmondsworth, 1961.
4. Cf. E. L. Mascall, *Existence & Analogy*, London, 1949, and especially Chapter 4.
5. Cf. A. M. Allchin, *The Dynamic of Tradition*, London, 1981 (p. 71). on the Scottish divine, James Sibbald (fl.c.1627).

Chapter Three

1. See R. Lane Fox, *Pagans and Christians*, Harmondsworth, 1986, Chapter 12, pp. 609ff.
2. See A. Kee, *Constantine versus Christ*, London, 1982. Kee draws together all possible negative judgements upon Constantine in this honestly polemical work.
3. The title of Chapter XI in G. Dix, *The Shape of the Liturgy*, Westminster, 1945, pp. 303–396.
4. See A. Schmemann, *Introduction to Liturgical Theology*, London, 1966, pp. 40–59 and Dix, *op. cit.*, 1945, p. 314.
5. P. Brown, *The Cult of the Saints*, London, 1981, p. 157.
6. P. Brown, *The Making of Late Antiquity*, Cambridge, Mass, and London, 1978, p. 95.
7. See P. Brown, *op. cit.*, 1978.
8. The sentence, 'He placed himself in the order of signs,' is taken from the conclusion of David Jones' important essay, *Art and Sacrament*; it is there attributed to Maurice de la Taille. See D. Jones, *Epoch and Artist*, London, 1959, p. 179.
9. Clement of Rome, *First Epistle to the Corinthians* XLI. The section XL–XLIV is relevant.
10. G. Dix, *op. cit.*, 1945, p. 436.
11. See R. P. C. Hanson, *Office and the Concept of Office in the Early Church*, Chapter 8 of *Studies in Christian Antiquity*, Edinburgh, 1985, pp. 128 and 131.

Chapter Four

1. Notably in St Augustine's thinking, cf. P. Brown, *Augustine of Hippo*, London, 1967, p. 352.
2. V. W. Turner, *The Ritual Process*, Harmondsworth, 1974.
3. See Turner, *op. cit.*, 1974, p. 119.
4. All who employ this pattern acknowledge its origin in A. van Gennep, *The Rites of Passage*, Chicago, 1960.

5. Turner, *op. cit.*, 1974, p. 81. The root of liminal is the Latin *limen*: threshold.
6. The sub-title of Turner's *The Ritual Process* is *Structure and Anti-Structure*.
7. Turner, *op. cit.*, 1974, p. 82, pp. 114–116 and p. 119 *et seq.*
8. Turner, *op. cit.*, 1974, pp. 95, 115.
9. Although Turner distinguishes marginality from liminality he also tends to associate them very closely as bearers of communitas. I would argue that this is true only of some kinds of marginality, and that marginal groups insofar as they have ritual significance for the whole of society are not, in that respect, marginal. The Church's task in society is precisely to provoke a certain kind of communitas while resisting marginality.
10. See Turner, *op. cit.*, 1974, p. 92.
11. P. Berger's *The Social Reality of Religion* is known in the USA as *The Sacred Canopy*.
12. See Turner, *op. cit.*, 1974, p. 193.
13. Turner, *op. cit.*, 1974, p. 166.

Chapter Five

1. Cf. I. & P. Opie, *The Lore and Language of Schoolchildren*, Oxford, 1959.
2. The title of R. C. Moberley's classic, *Ministerial Priesthood* (London, 1897) encapsulates this view, as the book itself expounds it. It is significant that he draws it out from NT christological images, showing how developing ideas of sacral priesthood in the church still derive their life from that source.
3. The word *symbol* is itself symbolic of a vast field of experience and so resists definition. F. W. Dillistone, *The Power of Symbols* (London 1986) offers a lengthy definition in the form 'an *a* which does *x*, for *b*' where *a* is concrete, *b* is transcendent and *x* represents a large range of signifying actions (p. 13).
4. C. R. Bryant, *The River Within*, London, 1978, pp. 24ff.
5. The idea that symbols participate in the reality they symbolise appears in Goethe and Coleridge and has become familiar in theology through the work of Paul Tillich and Karl Rahner. See Dillistone, *op. cit.*, chapters 2 and 7 and the literature referred to there.
6. Julian of Norwich, *Revelations of Divine Love*, translated by James Walsh, SJ, London 1961.
7. My use of the phrase 'intuition of being' derives from my reading of F. C. Copleston, SJ, *On Seeing and Noticing*, printed as Chapter 6 of his *Contemporary Philosophy*, London, 1956.
8. It is from this point of view that the question of the ordination of women is to be approached. A declaration which goes no further than to say that there is no substantial argument against it provides an insufficient basis for such a change. It suggests that the role of

theology could only be to allege impediments to a move which is desirable on non-theological grounds, and that it has been found wanting in its power to do that. The truth is that so significant a move is certainly theological in what it signifies, and the task of theologians is to elucidate and demonstrate this significance.

Chapter Six

1. Cf. F. C. Copleston, *Aquinas*, Harmondsworth, 1955, p. 87.
2. W. M. Abbot, SJ (ed.), *Documents of Vatican II*, London, 1967, p. 535.
3. Cf. J. Moltmann, *The Church in the Power of the Spirit*, London, 1977, pp. 126–130.
4. J. Macquarrie, *Principles of Christian Theology*, revised edition, London 1977, p. 425.
5. A point made by J. Moltmann, *The Church in the Power of the Spirit*, London, 1977, p. 303.
6. Typical of contemporary stress on 'all-member ministry' would be the interpretation of 2 Cor. 5.20, 'We are ambassadors, therefore, on behalf of Christ,' as referring to the whole church. Read in its context of fervent dispute between Paul and the Corinthian Church it is clear that 'we' here means Paul, who is fearful that rejection of his personal authority implies rejection of his gospel as well; cf. F. Young and D. Ford, *Meaning and Truth in 2 Corinthians*, London, 1987, pp. 71f.
7. Clement of Rome, *First Epistle to the Corinthians*, XLI.
8. See above, Chapter Three Note 8.
9. K. Rahner, *Foundations of Christian Faith*, London, 1978, pp. 411 *et seq.*
10. Article XXVI of the Thirty-Nine Articles of the Church of England.
11. U. Simon, *A Theology of Auschwitz*, London, 1967, p. 124.

Chapter Seven

1. Luther's Greater Catechism is printed, in English translation, in T. G. Tappert (tr. & ed.), *The Book of Concord*, Philadelphia, 1959, pp. 357 *et seq.* As this essay claims no originality in the field of Luther studies, I will not attempt to provide references to the Weimar Edition of Martin Luther's Works. Those disposed to seek the original content of my borrowings may do so, for the most part, in the volumes of the American Translation published by the Fortress Press, Philadelphia (LW) and in Gordon Rupp's *The Righteousness of God*, London, 1953.
2. G. Rupp, *op. cit.*, 1953, p. 299 says, 'In his later writings Luther speaks often of the "Three Hierarchies": The first is the Household, the second the State, the third the Church.' (*Of Councils and Churches* (1539) WA 50.652.)
3. G. Rupp, *op. cit.*, 1953, pp. 289, 293, 319.
4. *The Babylonian Captivity of the Church*, LW vol. 36, p. 70.
5. G. Rupp, op. cit., 1953, p. 201.

6. 'Before God' translates the latin *coram deo*, the phrase from which G. Rupp, op. cit., 1953, Part II takes its title.
7. *To the Christian Nobility*, LW vol. 44, p. 129.
8. *The Babylonian Captivity of the Church*, LW vol. 36, p. 116.
9. *The Babylonian Captivity of the Church*, LW vol. 36, p. 112; G. Rupp, *op. cit.*, 1953, p. 316. 'The priesthood of all the baptised', not 'all believers', must be recognised as the doctrine proper to Luther himself.
10. *The Babylonian Captivity of the Church*, LW vol. 36, p. 116; G. Rupp, *op. cit.*, 1953, p. 316.
11. G. Rupp, *op. cit.*, 1953, p. 263.
12. See G. Rupp, *op. cit.*, 1953, pp. 297–299.
13. Herbert's sensitivity to social change is perhaps most clearly declared in the lines

    Wherefore I dare not, I, put forth my hand
    To hold the Ark, although it seem to shake
    Through th' old sinnes and new doctrines of our Land;
    (*The Priesthood*)

    but one might also note the almost Marxian awareness of alienation in *Avarice*,

    Money . . .
    . . . thou hast got the face of man; for we
    Have with our stamp and seal transferred our right;

    and the early recognition that religion has become 'privatised' in *Decay*,

    But now Thou dost Thyself immure and close
    In some one corner of a feeble heart.

14. G. Rupp, *op. cit.*, 1953, p. 297.
15. See W. R. Graham, *The Constructive Revolutionary*, Richmond, 1971.

Chapter Eight

1. The theme of interaction with the context runs through W. Carr's *The Priestlike Task*, London, 1985. See especially pp. 5 *et seq.* Carr points out in several ways how inattention to this dimension or failure to understand it can lead to actions which exacerbate the problems they are meant to solve.
2. Cf. R. Gill, *Theology and Social Structure*, London, 1977, pp. 61f.
3. Cf. P. L. Berger, B. Berger and H. Kellner, *The Homeless Mind*, Harmondsworth, 1974, pp. 29 *et seq.*
4. Cf. T. Luckmann, *The Invisible Religion*, New York and London, 1967 p. 95.

5. T. Luckmann, *op. cit.*, 1967, pp. 97–99.
6. R. Dahrendorf, *The New Liberty*, London, 1975, p. 73.
7. T. Luckmann, *op. cit.*, 1967, p. 96.
8. P. Berger, *The Social Reality of Religion*, Harmondsworth, 1973, p. 138.
9. Berger, Berger and Kellner, *op. cit.*, 1974.
10. Berger, Berger and Kellner, *op. cit.*, 1974, pp. 44 *et seq.* The authors acknowledge a particular debt to Max Weber.
11. M. Hill makes particular use of the idea of 'revolution by tradition' in his *The Religious Order*, London, 1973, pp. 3 and 4 and passim.
12. J. Moltmann, *The 'Rose in the Cross of the Present'*, Chapter 5 of *Hope and Planning*, London 1971.
13. T. S. Eliot, *East Coker, III, in Collected Poems 1909–1962*, London, 1963, p. 200.
14. C. Wesley, Hymn 754 in *Hymns and Psalms*, London, 1983.
15. See A. Russell, *The Country Parish*, London, 1986, p. 271. The phrase points to the independence and authority which the priest needs to withstand local and personal pressures.

Chapter Nine

1. A. M. Ramsey, *The Gospel and the Catholic Church*, London, 1965, pp. 10, 28, 85.

Index of Subjects

Analogy 32f, 95f, 155
Angels 14, 73ff
Antistructure 59–72, 130
Apostleship 67, 91f, 94, 151
Askesis 148f
Atheism 131, 135, 157
Authority 12, 28f, 46, 66f, 74, 83, 91, 96, 123, 125, 143, 165

Baptism 37f, 48, 101, 103, 105, 121f
Bishop 52ff, 100f
Body of Christ 54, 96–8
Bureaucracy 137

Catholicity 111
Charismatic 20f, 97f
Clergy 16, 114, 122, 146
Consecration 14, 16, 36, 47, 87, 100, 105, 109, 154
Constantinian settlement 40–7, 167
Counter-reformation 125
Creeds 70, 83f
Cross of Christ 22, 30, 51, 81f, 152, 158, 163
Cult 35, 49, 52, 118
Culture 80, 87, 103, 112, 133f, 136, 157, 159

Daily Office 151f
Deacon 53, 100
Death 145, 165
Death of Christ 22, 35
Doctrine of Ministry 51, 82–6, 89f, 101, 108
Drudgery 116f
Dying & rising with Christ 35, 51, 87, 110f, 113, 122

Eastern Orthodoxy 15, 100
Ecclesi fasticism 123, 125, 142, 144, 162
Empathy 155f
Eschatology 42f, 104, 123
Eucharist 37, 40, 47–56, 77, 87, 98f, 102f, 105, 145f

Faith 11, 25, 30, 45, 75, 83ff, 102, 106, 126, 135, 139, 142ff, 156f
Fellowship 67, 132, 141
Freedom 23, 37, 79f, 121, 130, 135f, 142, 151
Function 112

Glory of God 88, 146, 161
Gospel 23, 28, 31, 37, 45, 55, 67f, 111
Grace 23, 25–8, 57, 83, 87f, 93, 95, 106–9, 113

Hebrews, epistle to 13, 17, 30–6, 51, 73, 148f, 153f, 158, 163
Heresy 44, 75
History 103f
Holiness 117f, 120, 123
Hope 2, 6, 23, 75, 79, 103f, 122, 161, 165
Humanity 3, 11, 14–18, 43, 68, 73–5, 103, 105, 120, 146f, 153, 158
Humanism 123–5

Idolatry 12, 15, 17, 56, 68, 157
Institution 7f, 11, 18, 20, 24, 27f, 37f, 42, 44, 50, 53, 55, 58, 62, 64f, 68f, 82, 85, 87, 97, 102, 110ff, 150
Interpretation 104, 145, 154

James, epistle of 27
John, gospel of 27, 76, 93f, 150
Jungian theory 78
Justification 8, 64, 72, 107–9, 120, 152

Kingdom of God 27, 47, 91, 93, 105, 127, 140, 144, 159, 162
Kingship 8, 17–22, 167

Laity 53f, 77, 94, 100f, 114–28, 142–7, 161
Language 31–5, 50, 52, 71, 162
Liberalism 37
Liminality 62–5, 168
Liturgy 13, 42f, 48, 53, 69, 76f, 89, 97
Luke, gospel of 27, 91f

Marginality 41, 43, 64, 168
Mark, gospel of 92
Marriage 65
Martyrs 45
Matthew, gospel of 27, 91ff
Metaphor 30–3
Middle Ages 110, 117ff, 123f
Miracle 108
Monks 45f, 119, 121, 159

Negative theology 15
New Testament 23–39, 43, 50–3, 114, 133

Ontology 112
Orders of Ministry 53, 96f, 99, 100
Ordination 89, 105, 109, 112, 163

Parents 4f, 57, 119f
Pastoral epistles 27
Pastoral ministry 75, 90, 97, 105
Paul, epistles of 26f, 28, 34f, 37, 51f, 63, 67, 85f, 88, 97f, 106f, 109, 151ff
Peter, first epistle of 34, 36, 51, 149
Pilgrimage 117, 119
Politics 18f, 21, 41, 46, 48, 120, 122, 131, 136, 138
Poor 92f
Pope 124
Power 3, 46, 52, 66, 99, 111, 140, 151
Prayer 89, 140, 149, 151, 161f, 164
Presidency 99f
Priesthood
- concept of 1–22, 144, 147, 149f, 152, 154, 158, 161
- eucharistic 47, 49f, 54f
- Israelite 3, 8, 18
- natural 3–6, 36
- New Testament language about 29–39
- of Christ 17–22, 31f, 51, 52
- of Church 9, 14, 34, 36, 52ff, 94, 99, 120, 130
- official 3f, 7
- of humanity 4, 6, 36, 130, 138, 158
- pagan 7, 52
- public status of 160
- sacral 3, 10, 17, 30, 40, 52, 54, 96, 129f, 158, 169

Private sphere 135, 138, 140, 158
Projection 18, 112, 167
Prophets 17, 20f
Providence 102f
Psalms 36

Rationality 5, 125, 134
Reconciliation 6
Reformation 114–28
Religion 3f, 12, 20, 23, 40, 49, 74, 79, 103, 132, 136, 140, 153
Renaissance 133
Representation 90–6, 108, 144, 155
Resurrection 107, 113
Revelation, book of 51
Revelation of God 12, 75, 91, 116, 125
Ritual 4, 6, 10, 63, 102, 163

Sacrament 13f, 37, 52, 77, 98f, 101–6, 147
Sacrifice 2, 34f, 51, 145
Schism 110f
Schoolchildren, lore of 74
Scripture 24, 37, 70, 83, 124
Secular 122, 126f, 131–47, 158, 164
Secularisation 131–47
Secularism 141
Servant 67, 95, 116f, 119, 121, 126, 150
Sex 154
Sign 98, 102, 109, 140
Society 3, 9f, 12, 16, 41, 46f, 54, 67, 78, 102, 113, 120f, 126, 129, 138
Sociology 55, 59, 113, 131, 140
Spirit of God 21, 34, 37f, 58, 67, 75f, 84, 94, 99, 104, 108, 129, 140, 151

Structure 24, 37, 55, 58, 62f, 65, 95, 130
Suffering 16, 65, 67, 147, 153ff
Symbol 9f, 13, 52, 69–72, 74, 77–82, 84, 87ff, 101, 104f, 111f, 143, 169
Synergy 107

Ten Commandments 120
Tradition 8f, 10, 20, 141
Trinity 100
Truth 11, 22, 45, 75, 103, 125, 127f

Unity of the Church 38, 44f, 47, 54, 96f, 110f

Vocation 108, 113, 121f, 131, 135, 142, 146f

Women, ordination of 169

Index of Names

Abbot W. M. 170
Allchin A. M. 168
Aquinas T. 123
Augustine of Hippo 168

Berger B. 171f
Berger P. 7f, 136, 167, 169, 171f
Brown P. 168
Bryant C. R. 77f, 169

Calvin J. 127
Carr W. 171
Clement of Rome 97, 168, 170
Coleridge S. T. 169
Constantine 40–47
Copleston F. C. 169f

Dahrendorf R. 135, 171
Darwin C. 157
Dillistone, F. W. 168f
Dix G. 40, 42f, 168

Eliot T. S. 23, 58, 145, 171
Empson W. 168
Erasmus D. 124

Farrer A. 167
Ford D. 170
Fowler H. W. 168
Freud S. 157

Gallienus 43
Galerius 43
Gennep A. van 168
Gill R. 171
Goethe J. W. von 169
Graham W. F. 171

Hanson R. P. C. 168
Herbert G. 115–17, 119, 126f, 171
Hill M. 171
Hitler A. 126
Holmes U. T. 167
Hopkins G. M. 87f

James E. O. 167
Jones D. 73, 102, 128, 168
Julian of Norwich 80f, 169

Keble J. 117
Kee A. 167f
Kellner H. 171f
Kierkegaard S. 159

Lane Fox R. 168
Luckmann T. 136, 167, 171f
Luther M. 95, 119–29, 131, 143, 170f

Machiavelli N. 124
Mackinnon D. 167
Macquarrie J. 96, 170
Marx K. 157
Mascall E. L. 168
Moberley R. C. 169
Moltmann J. 141, 167, 170f

Ollenburger B. C. 167
Opie I. & P. 169

Rahner K. 104, 169, 170
Ramsey A. M. 165, 171
Rupp, G. 170f
Russell A. 171

Sanders E. P. 168
Schmemann A. 42, 168
Sibbald J. 168
Simon U. 87, 110, 170
Spark M. 164

Taille M. de la 102, 168
Tarkovsky A. 1
Thomas R. S. 57

Tillich P. 169
Turner V. W. 61–3, 168f

Walsh J. 169

Wesley C. 171
Wesley J. 115

Young F. 170

'all dealings with God depends on the reality of the priesthood!

Priest

activities of priesthood act out + are an interpretation of life

make explicit 'official' that which is universal

priests represent that which society finds most significant

how does Tim 'act out' the gospel?

what's his interpretation

we're so out + live symbols - ceremonial life

"official" priesthood important as the foundation for "official" priesthood.

skills not instrumental rather to help people answer the question what is the point?

religious functionary

clear centre

diffuse edges

being exact is limiting

someone who can use their knowledge to put a name to the mystery

to stand beside people in their uncertainty

rehearse promises p6

bring assurance p6

affirm unity p6

interpret chance happenings as part of rational order

meet emergencies with hope p6

social role of priesthood

reconciler

help us to see our particularity in the context of the whole

liturgy the spirits

offering people a chance to share in the fun.

Priesthood must remain in touch with humanity